NET FLICKS

India's Smashing Affair
with the Shuttle

Akshay Lokapally &
Vijay Lokapally

Foreword by
Pullela Gopi Chand

B L O O M S B U R Y
NEW DELHI • LONDON • OXFORD • NEW YORK • SYDNEY

BLOOMSBURY INDIA
Bloomsbury Publishing India Pvt. Ltd
Second Floor, LSC Building No. 4, DDA Complex, Pocket C – 6 & 7,
Vasant Kunj, New Delhi, 110070

BLOOMSBURY, BLOOMSBURY INDIA and the Diana logo
are trademarks of Bloomsbury Publishing Plc

First published in India 2025
This edition published 2025

Copyright © Akshay Lokapally and Vijay Lokapally, 2025
Foreword copyright © Pullela Gopi Chand, 2025

Akshay Lokapally and Vijay Lokapally have asserted their right under the
Indian Copyright Act to be identified as the Authors of this work

All rights reserved. No part of this publication may be reproduced or transmitted in
any form or by any means, electronic or mechanical, including photocopying,
recording or any information storage or retrieval system, without prior
permission in writing from the publishers

This book is solely the responsibility of the authors and the publisher has had no
role in the creation of the content and does not have responsibility for anything
defamatory or libellous or objectionable

ISBN: PB: 978-93-56407-07-7; eBook: 978-93-56409-41-5
2 4 6 8 10 9 7 5 3 1

Typeset in Adobe Garamond by Manipal Technologies Limited
Printed and bound in India by Gopsons Papers Pvt. Ltd., Noida

To find out more about our authors and books visit www.bloomsbury.com and sign
up for our newsletters

ADVANCE PRAISE FOR *NET FLICKS*

'As president of the Badminton Association of India, I have witnessed the immense dedication and hard work required to excel in this sport. Akshay and Vijay Lokapally's *Net Flicks* beautifully chronicles the journey of Indian badminton, highlighting the grit and glory of our players. This inspiring book captures the essence of the sport and the dreams of countless aspiring shuttlers'
  Dr Himanta Biswa Sarma, chief minister of Assam and president of Badminton Association of India

'As someone who has covered Indian sports for over five decades, I am truly impressed by the depth and insight offered in *Net Flicks*. Akshay and Vijay Lokapally provide an unparalleled account of the game's growth in India, paying tribute to the pioneers and modern stars who have inspired millions. Their work is a significant contribution to the chronicles of Indian sports history'
  S. Thyagarajan, veteran sports journalist

'Badminton is not just a sport; it's a test of endurance, strategy, and heart. When I look at how the game has grown in India, especially with today's champions inspiring millions, it fills me with immense pride. What was once a niche pursuit has become a national passion. *Net Flicks* beautifully captures that journey, the dedication of players, and the spirit of an entire nation rallying behind the shuttle'
  Ami Ghia, former international badminton player and Arjuna awardee

'I am pleased to note that Akshay and Vijay Lokapally have collaborated to write a book on badminton in India, focusing on stars of the past. This release comes at a time when badminton has made impressive progress. I wish them both all the best'
  Dinesh Khanna, former Asian badminton champion

Net Flicks

To late Nandu Natekar, for inspiring a generation of players

Contents

Foreword by Pullela Gopi Chand   xi
Introduction   1

1. Prakash Nath: Pioneering the Path of Dedication   7
2. Nandu Natekar: The Genesis of Indian Badminton   14
3. Dinesh Khanna: Triumphs and Trials   24
4. Trailblazers of the Past: Women's Badminton in the Mid-20th Century   34
5. Damayanti Tambay: Grace on the Court   41
6. Arif Saab: Crafting Legends Through Coaching   49
7. Prakash Padukone: The Iconic Master   57
8. Syed Modi: A Star's Shining Legacy   68
9. Ameeta Singh: Breaking Barriers with Every Smash   76
10. Ami Ghia: Magic on the Court   88
11. Kanwal Thakar Singh: Shaping the Court with Strength   97
12. Hufrish Nariman: The Charming Dissenter   107
13. Leroy D'Sa: The Steadfast Support   112
14. Manjusha Kanwar: Conquering Courts with Courage   126
15. Madhumita Bisht: A Feathered Fury   138
16. Pullela Gopi Chand: Architect of Indian Badminton Renaissance   148
17. Aparna Popat: The Queen of the Court   159
18. Jwala Gutta: Rebel with a Cause   171
19. Ashwini Ponnappa: Silent Warrior   178
20. Saina Nehwal: Epitome of Determination   182
21. P. V. Sindhu: The Swift Conqueror   188
22. Behind the Scenes: Unsung Heroes of Indian Badminton   193
23. Game Changers: Evolution of Badminton Leagues in India   197
24. State of the Shuttle: Navigating the Currents of Indian Badminton   205

Acknowledgements   211
Index   213
About the Authors   217

Foreword

IT HAS BEEN A remarkable journey for Indian badminton, from the early years when aspiring professionals had to overcome a lack of facilities to the current era when our players have access to the best training, equipment and infrastructure. This progress is a testament to the resilience and determination of our players, coaches, federation and government, who have all played pivotal roles at different stages.

I was attracted to badminton because it was not a contact sport like football or hockey. Badminton tests not only one's mental and physical abilities but also their character. The suppleness of a player's body is as crucial as their endurance. The sport teaches respect for the opponent. You may lose a long rally, but that does not stop you from nodding in appreciation. I have never had any inhibitions of conceding that my opponent may have played better than me.

I grew up in Hyderabad hearing stories about the stalwarts of Indian badminton – the likes of Nandu Natekar, Dinesh Khanna, Prakash Padukone and Syed Modi, to name a few. I learned the game under the guidance of Syed Mohammed Arif and Hamid Hussain. During his time as the chief national coach, Arif Saab contributed considerably to badminton in our country and deserves a special mention in any story about badminton in India.

Badminton is an indoor sport that offers unique challenges. We only sometimes got to train in the indoor halls, where the tournaments were mostly played. However, our badminton community is a tightly knit unit and each player's progress is closely monitored. This support system helps the development of young talent and is also an excellent resource for established players.

Badminton brings joy to Indian sports lovers who enjoy seeing our nation's athletes excel internationally. Indian badminton players winning medals at various international events continue to boost the sport's popularity domestically. We have seen a massive increase in the number of youngsters dreaming of making it big in badminton. I am also glad to see the sport being taken up even in remote corners of the country.

One of the main reasons badminton is growing in popularity is the possibility of a full-time career. With an increasing number of academies being established, there are more employment opportunities for those connected with the game. Coaches, players, and equipment manufacturers have much to gain from the ecosystem around the sport. The increasing revenue generated from this growth augurs well for the sport in the country.

I must acknowledge the support of the Sports Authority of India (SAI) and the Sports Ministry for introducing various tournaments at the junior level. Apart from this systematic training of youngsters, there is support from the Badminton Association of India (BAI) for them to gain international exposure by playing in tournaments abroad. We have also benefited from the services of foreign coaches at different times. It is heartening to see that there is a concerted effort by the BAI and the SAI to identify future champions.

In India, players also benefit from family and parental support. I take this opportunity to acknowledge the role played by parents of young athletes, not just in badminton but in every sport. The support system at home goes a long way in helping an individual achieve their goal. My mother, Subbaravamma, has been my guiding force. She helped me live my dreams by making many sacrifices in her own life. Parents are as important as coaches in the success of an athlete.

Foreword

In my younger days, reports on badminton were limited to one or two paragraphs in the national newspapers. This has changed now – there are articles and columns focused on the sport, a remarkable transformation from when badminton struggled to find mention in the media. However, even though badminton is growing in popularity in our country, the literature on the sport does not match its stature.

That is why writing the foreword to this book gives me immense joy. This is a collaboration between Vijay and Akshay Lokapally, a father-son duo. I know Vijay as a veteran cricket writer, and I was impressed by Akshay's efforts to travel around the country to meet the badminton champions of yesteryears. I am happy that they have brought us stories of famous and little-known names in Indian badminton.

A lot of hard work has gone into gathering the material for this book. The book's attention to women badminton players, who often remain in the background, adds a unique perspective to the narrative. Storytelling in sports is essential to make people aspire to become like the stars. Chronicling their journey is important. Vijay has extensively covered the sport and its growth over the years, so I do not doubt that this book will significantly contribute to the story of Indian badminton for years to come.

Knowing Vijay and the enthusiasm of Akshay, I am sure readers can look forward to exciting stories as the book celebrates India's fabulous badminton journey.

I congratulate Vijay, Akshay and Bloomsbury India for this welcome effort to give badminton the importance it deserves. I wish the book all the best, and I pray this will be one of many.

Pullela Gopi Chand
Padma Bhushan awardee
Chief coach of the Indian national badminton team
Winner of the All-England Open Badminton Championship

Introduction

SUMMITS ARE MEANT TO be scaled. Mount Everest has been a fascinating attraction for climbers for many generations. The sporting peaks beckon their respective champions to conquer them. Every sport has a challenge. All of them are monumental. There is intrigue and demand for your skills and endurance as you pursue excellence, whether it be on the turf, the court or the field. Indian sport has come a long way and now has arrived at a stage where a podium finish, not mere participation, is the goal.

Cricket and hockey have held the masses' attention. There was promise from football, too, but India has yet to make an international impact in it, even though it has been considered a sleeping giant for some time now. Hockey has managed its position through sporadic titles, while cricket has grabbed the most extensive support from the fans and media.

Badminton has emerged as a new hope in the mind of the masses. Over the years, it provided cherished moments for fans through the achievements of players like Nandu Natekar, Dinesh Khanna, Prakash Padukone, Syed Modi and Pullela Gopi Chand. These players defied challenges from well-equipped overseas competitors and became champions in international tournaments. They also stood up against counterproductive practices enforced by Indian administrators.

S. Thyagarajan of *The Hindu*, a veteran writer, deserves credit for regularly highlighting the problems of the players in their fight against the federation. Stalwarts like

Padukone suffered at the hands of officials who denied players the opportunity to grow and plan their financial security.

Thyagarajan, writing in *Sportstar*, highlighted the players' complaints about the lack of incentives and deplorable facilities during the tournaments. He urged the organisers to be more open to the players' requests for more prize money tournaments. Padukone wanted the administrators to rope in top industrial houses to look at boosting the players' financial returns.

Surprisingly, the federation would not inform Padukone about the invitations he received for overseas tournaments. Thyagarajan revealed that the federation wanted Padukone to participate in local competitions and kept him unaware of the international invitations.

Padukone's historic win at the All-England title in 1980 and his world number 1 ranking inspired the youth and brought joy to thirsty fans. Gopi Chand emulated this feat in 2001. They both stand as the first Indians to clinch the prestigious All-England crown.

If Padukone then was the face of Indian badminton, Gopi Chand is the modern reflection of the game. Both have a striking similarity. They backed themselves on the faith their fans had in them and amazingly adapted to the challenges by making great strides. Remarkably, Padukone travelled the world on his terms, even though he had to struggle for financial support to participate in tournaments abroad. His self-belief was a fantastic trait.

Gopi Chand followed Padukone's footsteps and left a mark on the game by making his presence felt in the international circuit. He fought a crippling knee injury to chart his journey. Gopi understood the nuances of modern badminton at various stages of his career and studied them deeply to emerge as an authority on the game. He has been an important part of the schemes that the Union government has formulated to encourage badminton at the grassroots level, as well as the expertise needed at the elite stage.

There has been a revolution in women's badminton with some spectacular performances by P. V. Sindhu and Saina Nehwal. V. V. Subrahmanyam of *The Hindu* and *Sportstar* has closely followed the careers of Saina and Sindhu since they took the early steps. 'There is no doubt that it was the inspirational journey of Saina which led many like Sindhu to get a feel of what it means to be a successful badminton player, particularly at a time when the sport was just getting noticed, again thanks to Saina's spectacular achievements,' says Subrahmanyam. For some time, the careers of Saina and Sindhu ran parallel before the former slowly faded away, but not before leaving an indelible impression on the sport. They are contrasting personalities in many ways – physique, playing style and their on-court mannerisms.

On the flip side, Sindhu's early days in the circuit were a testament to her dominating personality – a force to reckon with both on and off the court. The lanky shuttler became synonymous with her awe-inspiring smashes, a trait she might have inherited from her parents – Arjuna awardee P. V. Ramana and P. Vijaya, who represented India in volleyball.

There is little to separate these two champion shuttlers regarding court movement. The big difference is that Saina often pulled off sensational wins while Sindhu faltered quite frequently during the tense moments of a decider – perhaps caught in the dilemma of whether to attack or defend.

For Sindhu, the support came from her father, a noted volleyball player of his time. Saina, too, gained from the encouragement she got from her father. The parents of Sindhu and Saina have had considerable roles in them reaching the heights of the sport by winning Olympic medals and inspiring a generation of players to dream big.

In earlier eras, players such as the Apte sisters, the Deodhar sisters, Meena Shah, Suresh Goel, and Leroy D'Sa were mentioned repeatedly – some for their style and some for their capacity to play hours on the court! The tenacious spirit of these veterans was the reason the game flourished.

What if the international titles eluded the Indians? They prevailed on their own. There was no television, and that was a pity. Those who watched Goel, Trilok Nath Seth, Prakash Nath, Natekar and Ami Ghia raved about their presence on the court. There is very little video footage of these stars during their youth.

The modern achievers have gained from the work of the past masters. Saina and Sindhu had role models in Ami, Madhumita, and Manjusha Kanwar for their hard work and longevity. Aparna Popat is a modern great in Indian badminton. However, only some can claim the status Saina and Sindhu have carved for themselves.

Media attention meant the players had to be at their best. Expectations grew manifold as Saina and Sindhu ruled the stage. Even as Saina showed the way, they had to contend with the Chinese. Sindhu was more consistent, which worked well for the badminton fraternity.

The turning point came when Saina won the bronze at the 2012 London Olympics. Suddenly, there was a surge in girls wanting to play badminton. Academies sprung up in various cities to meet the demands of parents who wanted their girls to take up badminton as a career. When Sindhu won a silver, the first by an Indian woman, at the 2016 Rio Olympics, it was the trigger for badminton to grow big.

Acknowledging the efforts of the badminton players, the Union government made a huge investment by launching the Target Olympic Podium Scheme (TOPS) and including badminton as a priority sport. Funds were generously made available for the players to train abroad and keep them focused by competing judiciously.

TOPS, aided by the vision of the Badminton Association of India (BAI), was the reason for the game's mass appeal, and with players winning more and more titles overseas, it was time for the coaches to make a mark by consistently performing and figuring in the top ten in their groups.

With youngsters participating more in the domestic circuit, badminton saw a welcome increase in prize money tournaments and individual sponsorships. It was a fantastic development that badminton players started engaging personal managers to boost their financial returns through sponsorships. Managers were no longer the domain of cricketers, golfers, footballers and tennis stars.

The success on the court created a healthy system where top-class facilities for the players bore encouraging results. It reached its pinnacle in 2022 when India made history by winning the Thomas Cup. From the best of a semifinal slot in the seventy-three-year-history of the tournament, the Indian team won the crown in Bangkok by beating fourteen-time champions Indonesia. The 3–0 margin reflected India's magnificent domination, led by the young Lakshya Sen, Kidambi Srikanth, and the doubles pair of Chirag Shetty and Satwiksairaj Rankireddy.

Chirag and Satwik also became the first Indians to win a Badminton World Federation World Tour event at all levels from Super 100 to 1000. It was in keeping with their remarkable progress that they won the doubles in the Indonesia Open, beating the Malaysian world champion pair of Aaron Chia and Soh Wooi Yik on 18 June 2023. It was a proud moment for the nation when they were crowned the Asian champions. A month later, Satwik was credited with the Guinness world record for the fastest smash recorded at 565 kmph, improving upon the previous best of 493 kmph by Malaysia's Tan Boon Heong in 2013.

Indian women clinching a historic gold in the Asia Team Championships in February 2024 proved the improving quality of the game and its increasing popularity among the youth. Sindhu, Anmol Kharb, Tressa Jolly and Gayatri Gopi Chand pulled off an incredible 3–2 victory over Thailand. True, Thailand was without its top two singles players – Ratchanok Intanon and Pornpawee Chochuwong – but nothing should take away the credit from the young Indian team. The hero of the triumph was seventeen-year-old Anmol from Faridabad, who won over world number 45 Pornpicha Choeikeewong in the decider.

This book celebrates the journey of Indian badminton from its humble beginnings to its present glory.

1

Prakash Nath: Pioneering the Path of Dedication

IN CRICKET-CRAZY INDIA, badminton has emerged as the second most popular sport, with achievements in the Olympics, Asian Games, Commonwealth Games and World Championships to stir the imagination of sports lovers.

In 1934, Vijay Madgavkar earned the distinction of becoming the first singles national champion. The following year, T. Banerji won the title. Then, the singles trophy was won by George Lewis for four consecutive years. According to badminton player and historian, Shirish Nadkarni, Lewis also won the mixed doubles crown with his wife, Nobina. In fourteen years of participation, Lewis collected ten titles. Sadly, badminton events would mostly go unreported at that time. The arrival of Prakash Nath and Davinder Mohan in the early 1940s was an era of magic on the court where the media took notice and highlighted their healthy rivalry.

Nath's story is a poignant one. He watched his world crumble in one moment of grief. 'Lahore in Flames', screamed the headline in a London newspaper as he went for a stroll on the morning of his All-England Badminton Championship final against Conny Jepsen of Denmark. His city and house were burning and, shockingly, he had no news of his family's wellbeing.

It was not the scenario when he had left the shores of his beloved nation. Badminton was close to his heart. So were his family members. He should have been by their side in those miserable times. Little could he have imagined this dark chapter in India's history where friends turned foes and neighbours went for each other's throats. At twenty-three, Nath was thousands of miles from his home in Lahore. India and Pakistan, having attained independence from British rule, celebrated their newly achieved status by rioting in the streets.

Badminton was the last thing on his mind as he faced Jepsen. In their previous encounter, he had beaten the Dane, but this was not a test of his badminton skills. His mental resilience was being challenged, and he was destined to fail on a stage which, sadly, he vowed never to revisit. Nath lost the final and, with it, his zeal for the game which he loved so much. Badminton was his life. Not anymore. It was now the last thing he cared about. He wanted to return home and reunite with his family.

'I almost lost my life on several occasions during those dreadful days, and they gave me nightmares for years after that. Badminton went far away from my mind; my priority became my survival. I vowed not to touch a badminton racquet again, until my once-thriving family business had been rejuvenated,' Nath revealed in an interview.

Nath grew up in Lahore with dreams of achieving great heights in badminton. He was talented enough to impact the world stage, and the trip to London for the All-England Championships was set to create an unforgettable chapter in his life. It did. The trip snatched badminton from him even though he had made the title round.

Not born into a family of badminton lovers, Nath's love for the game started at eight when he wandered into one of the many rooms in their sprawling home and discovered a racquet. It was love at first sight for Nath, and the racquet became his new friend. His father, Lok Nath, a hockey star, provided crucial support as Nath's passion for badminton developed into an obsession. There was no formal training, but his aspirations led the way. His training sessions were at the makeshift court built at home for the youngster. He picked the nuances of the game by learning on his own. His father's support made a huge difference.

'The house buzzed with youngsters in our joint family, providing an abundance of players who organised impromptu tennis and table tennis competitions within the family. The boys achieved remarkable heights, and it deserves applause. Formal training was a luxury they didn't have in Lahore,' his daughter, Ratna, shared.

Nath showcased his talent early on. He clinched his maiden national title at the age of sixteen in 1942, including the doubles with his elder brother, Ashok. The following two years saw him lose the title to Devinder Mohan, only to reclaim it in 1945. However, Mohan once again secured the championship in 1946. Their journey led them to qualify for the All-England Championship in 1947, where a twist of fate pitted them against each other in the quarterfinals.

The draw pitted Nath and Mohan against each other in the quarterfinals. They made a surprising decision not to compete against each other, leaving both the British media and badminton enthusiasts stunned. They settled the contest by tossing the coin, preserving energy for the semifinal. Nath won the toss, smashed his opponent, a British challenger named Redford in the semifinal, and set up a clash for the title with Jepsen.

The performance of Nath at All-England was even more incredible because he and Mohan had had no time to prepare for the trip. Back then, things like training camps were unheard of, and the players often had to rush into the tournament without professional preparation. In this case, Nath and Mohan learnt of their trip a mere four days before the tournament.

According to Nath's daughter, Ratna, he did not have the best equipment. 'He told me once that a racquet string snapped, and he had to fix it without professional support.' Travelling to London was tiring, with stops in Lahore, Cairo and Rome before finally reaching their destination. Despite the exhaustion, their motivation to play kept them going. When they were handed the competition draw upon their arrival, Nath and Mohan realised that they were set to meet in the quarterfinals. They were so confident of overcoming their opponents that eventually they kept their appointment.

The organisers were surprised that Nath had taken for granted his win against a former champion, Tage Madsen of Denmark, even before they had played. Nath won 7–15, 15–12, 15–3. He eliminated Ireland's Tod Majury 15–7, 15–11 in the next round. It was clear that Nath was in the best form of his life.

Having reached the quarterfinals, Nath and Mohan faced the dilemma of how to win the contest without tiring each other out. The two were long-time friends and opponents in Lahore and understood each other's game too well. They worried the match would leave them physically exhausted and short of stamina for the final.

The decision to decide the winner by the toss of a coin underlined the importance Nath and Mohan gave to the fact that one of them had to face the opponent with a fresh state of mind and body.

Ratna recalled the day of the final was notable for her father. She said, 'He had taken the win for granted because he was in such awesome form. But he was devastated when he heard of the happenings back home, and his mind went blank on the court. He said he froze on the court. I learnt he led initially, but the images of his house in flames and people butchering each other in the worst communal riots ever left him shattered. He lost tamely (7–15, 11–15).

We were told later that he could have won the match comfortably. He had the game to become the champion but not the fate to seal it.'

As badminton historian Nadkarni describes, 'Agility was his forte; and when he bent his back to hit an overhead shot, the racquet was reputed to touch the back of his heel. He was also a master of deception, with a rich repertoire of strokes, especially at the net.'

Heartbroken and disillusioned, Nath returned to Lahore to discover a world he never could have visualised in his lifetime. There was widespread looting and killing on the streets. Lahore was a burning city like never before. 'My dad narrated a chilling story of his escape to India. I still shiver when I recall it. There was no communication between my dad and the rest of the family. The women folk had fled to India, but his brother stayed in Lahore, hoping my dad would return. He did. But he also nearly lost his life.'

Nath and his brother, Ashok, left for Amritsar in their Fiat car, which broke down halfway through the journey. Ratna recalls, 'There was an army convoy moving to Amritsar, and my dad and his brother knew the commanding officer. The car broke down, but the convoy kept moving. The officer realised much later. However, he promised my dad and uncle that he would return quickly after ordering the convoy to halt. In the meantime, those who were fleeing India surrounded the car. There was a real threat as they assaulted my dad and other occupants of the car before the army officer reached with a few jawans and saved them. They fixed the car in the nick of time, and my father and uncle survived to tell the story to us.'

The Nath family left behind a vast collection of trophies won in Lahore in a room. 'Years later, in the 1990s, one of my cousins visited Lahore to see if any memorabilia was to be found in the house. Some paintings by my aunts were also left behind. Would you believe it? Refugees had taken over the house from India, and one of the youngsters happened to discover the racquets. My dad said the boy became a national-level player in Pakistan. Sadly, I don't remember the boy's name, but my father was glad that the badminton equipment was put to good use,' Ratna recalled.

The once affluent Nath family lived the life of refugees in India. Badminton was the last thing on Nath's mind. It never returned to his life. 'My dad had the responsibility of settling down. He had sisters to marry off. He was thirty-two when he was forced to marry. He met my mother at a party. He never played badminton after leaving Lahore. He did not even teach me. He followed the sport, and I remember he was invited to an event by the Federation when Padukone won the All-England title. I remember seeing the newspaper clipping many years later with the headline Prakash meets Prakash. I think that was his only association with the game after that sad day in London,' said Ratna.

Starting from scratch, Nath sought shelter in a hen pen in Delhi and set up a machine tools factory on the plot of land that came his way. Nath was known for his hard work; he would not return home for days as he grappled with various hardships. 'Picture this – a badminton player making tools for the Indian Railways. The food trays that you saw on the trains were his products. He would make utensils from waste and generously give them to the staff. He was a kind-hearted man. He never harmed an ant in his life. Soft-spoken, I never saw him angry. All he would say was, "Not done". He finally built his house in 1974 and was thrilled at it. He just wanted us to do well.'

Ratna said, 'A doting father, he allowed us to pursue our love for music. He did not insist we become sportspersons, though. But we loved sports. He was at his best when we went on an annual holiday to Kashmir. We did it for sixteen years. We also had a household help who my mother initiated into education. Hailing from a village in Garhwal, he studied in ITI (Indian Technology Institute) and joined my dad's factory. My dad was thrilled to see him travel overseas and become a supervisor.'

In later years, Nath spent his free time playing golf. He never returned to the badminton court after competing in the All-England final with a broken racquet.

2

Nandu Natekar: The Genesis of Indian Badminton

NANDU NATEKAR WAS ONLY ten when he started playing badminton in the small town of Sangli, Maharashtra. This was the right age to choose and begin a sport, but he also gave his parents a reason for agony. It is easier to find an interest when the anxiety of one's future is at bay. Biology, too, has your back then. What's important is getting the necessary support to groom oneself. Natekar would play at the Sangli Gymkhana – a sanctuary for the one with a love for sports – which played a crucial role in shaping his early career and passion for sports.

Popular internet definitions describe a gymkhana as a place of assembly. It is a centre for holding contests to display one's skill, mainly in sports. The term, known to have originated in Persia, was adopted by the British to create gentlemen's clubs, later known for their social gatherings, sporting culture and etiquette.

The game was not veiled; children and young adults alike would be spotted in compounds of independent houses, open grounds, or lawns with racquets in their hands. For children, it was an easy decision when the question of choosing a game or a sport for the evening would arise. Equipment to indulge in an easy-to-play game was accessible. A racquet and a 'phool' (shuttlecock) were all they needed. They would make do with whatever space they could find, and narrow alleys between buildings were capitalised on too. The younger lot created their version using plastic bats. Still, it failed miserably at occupying the house kitchens, which delighted the mothers' fraternity. However, when it meant choosing badminton as a career option, it could not be called a common man's sport. One needed access to clubs and gymkhanas to be recognised as a blooming talent in the sport. And that was available to the middle class and above. It is hard to find players who despite not having club memberships were able to forge their way into the top brass of badminton. There came many who took advantage of such opportunity and Natekar was not far behind. His passion for the sport made him submit himself to its arduous demands.

Natekar's mischief, also a cause of his opponent's pain, was not limited to the court. Initially, it took him a lot of work to enter the local gymkhana. But he couldn't care any less and would sneak in. Also, having the privilege of his grandfather being the president of the gymkhana, he was at least allowed in. The regulars protested, but soon, it turned into a joyous hail. They were cheering for Natekar. Not knowing how far he would go with his talent but delighted by his game, they accepted him.

They had to offer him a special membership as, by law, he was a junior. But it didn't take long for him to start challenging the seniors and for them to regret the day they stopped the protests! He was granted membership after showing his game's appeal and demonstrating the promise of talent. Natekar always felt fortunate to have been born into a family interested in sports. And badminton held a special place among the rest.

Natekar's father was a fan of racquet sports and mainly took an interest in tennis. Serving as the superintendent of the post office, he and his family had to go through the usual unease and joys that come with moving constantly. But sports was in their DNA. His grandfather owned the local gymkhana – Desai Pavilion – for which he had to invest ₹5,500, a hefty sum.

Natekar's uncles and cousins were regulars on the badminton courts and their neighbours enjoyed playing too. All of which made Natekar even more inclined to take up sports. Baroda, Ahmedabad, Dharwad and Ratnagiri were a few provinces where tournaments were held.

It was the 1940s, and inter-school tournaments were unheard of when racquets were made out of wood, and the strings were different from the synthetic ones commonly used now. The most popular of those was the Maxply Dunlop. Racquets today weigh somewhere between 75 to 85 grams. But back then they weighed around 140 to 150 grams, almost double. This limited the opportunities to play and showcase skills on the courts worldwide. One had to rely on one's gift of deception, if one had it, or on one's strength to make one's opponent think twice before deciding on a return. One is reminded of the Chinese players who achieved prominence much later because of this. They were known to embody the famous saying 'means to an end'. Racquets would come and go, but the game never stopped.

'It is all about adapting to the circumstances. If players from olden times were given lighter racquets, then they would have shaped their game and style accordingly. And if today's players were also offered heavier racquets when they were young, they too would acclimatise to the bulk of those racquets,' says Nadkarni, a veteran journalist and a badminton historian. He goes on to echo Natekar's words, 'A champion player will be a champion in any era. She will adapt to the prevailing conditions effortlessly.'

Matches in India at that time were played on 'Shahabadi' flooring, which was made with puzzle-like tiles. This style could also be seen on streets and pavements. And there were times when matches were held on mud courts. The racquets were heavy and courts were not kind to the knees. All the state and national level tournaments were played with the net set at a fixed height. Even back then, the net was at a height of five feet one inch at the edges and leaned towards five feet at the centre, where it tends to sag a little bit. There was a proper way to position the net.

All representative tournaments used a stick of height five feet one inch which served the purpose of a ruler. The stick was held vertically at the centre point of the net to fix it at the required height. The stick had two markings, one right at the top and the second one inch below that. The second mark helped to hold the centre of the net at five feet. Affixing the net too tight meant the centre would move up by an inch and this used to prove disadvantageous to players whose shots were accurate to a decimal place. A difference of even half an inch could change the course of the match for them. And Natekar was amongst those who believed in extreme precision.

Shirish Nadkarni shares an anecdote which he treats as a fond memory of Natekar's style and stroke-play. It was 1967 when Nadkarni was playing the double's final in junior nationals. After being beaten, he and his partner advanced to serve as linesmen for the game afterwards. It was a doubles match in which Natekar was paired with Gautam Thakkar. The pair was not a favourite because Thakkar was an outstanding singles player but a modest one at doubles. They lost the first game 11–15 and were trailing 6–12 in the second. That's when Thakkar went up to Natekar and pleaded with him to do something spectacular. Natekar was cool and composed. 'He asked him if he wanted to win. On getting an affirmative, he only asked Thakkar to execute the service and manage the net well. Natekar wanted the rest of the court to himself,' recalls Nadkarni.

One particular shot that was witnessed by a packed audience at Matunga Gymkhana with about 250 spectators was when one of the opposing players, Godse, raised the shuttle cross-court from his backhand net corner to Natekar's backhand net corner. He returned it the first time to the same point from where Godse had sent it. 'The shuttle was about an inch over the net. Natekar returned it once more making the shuttle gravitate even closer to the net. Then Natekar's third return stunned the audience and the gymkhana roared with their thunderous claps, when the shuttle just rolled over the tape,' Nadkarni remembers with astounding details. They made an unbelievable comeback in the second game and were 18–15 and clinched the match by winning the third 15–6. The match was completely controlled by Natekar.

Natekar moved to Bombay and was admitted to Ruia College, one of the country's most reputed institutions for higher education. He started playing matches at the inter-university level. He would attend lectures in the morning, reach the courts by afternoon and spend the rest of the evening practising. In no time, he proved himself with his craft. Natekar soon secured membership to the prestigious Hindu Gymkhana and began playing at the state level. There was no distinction made between professionals and amateurs. If a player was invited to participate in a tournament outside their hometown, they would only be reimbursed for their travel and a night's stay. There was no pay or cash prizes. Status is what builds careers and dethrones the masters. But it was innocently absent from badminton then. The absence of prestige helped bring raw talent to the fore, with games played only to quench one's thirst for the game.

There were about seven or eight annual tournaments held in Bombay at the time, and each year saw a growing number of entries and spectators. It forbode the incremental passion that the nation was about to feel for the sport. Not forgetting the efforts by the Bombay State Association,

Natekar recalls, 'Badminton had picked momentum in Bombay then.' The association popularised the sport by launching a few more tournaments in the city.

In 1953, Natekar represented the province of Bombay at the national tournament in Gwalior. It was Natekar's second appearance at the competition. His first appearance the previous year at Lucknow had seen him exit in the first round. But this time, Natekar defeated the much revered and feared Trilok Nath Seth to clinch the singles title. From then on, the clashes between these two would be highly anticipated as they promised a spectacle.

No fan who came to watch their rivalry unfold slowly on the court ever returned dissatisfied. Natekar also won the mixed doubles with Shashi Bhat. He would win both titles the following year as well. He won the doubles title, partnering with Ravindra Dongre in 1955 and R. D. Vimawala in 1956. After two successive singles titles, his most challenging adversary, T. N. Seth, won for three consecutive years, denying Natekar the title until 1958.

The two were so popular that spectators once turned hostile after being denied entry to a match between them in Guwahati. When they were told that tickets were sold out, they began pelting stones at the stadium. In the end, Seth and Natekar had to request the officials and the seated spectators to accommodate the upset ones outside. People were seated on the floor, stairs and even a few inches from the lines delineating the court!

During Natekar's time, players from northern India would dominate the badminton circuit. Seth and other successful contemporaries, such as Amrit Lal Diwan, Parduman Chawla and S. L. Jaini, were from north India. Natekar challenged that monopoly and became the only one from Maharashtra to win multiple singles titles. Apart from his previous wins, 1958 saw his return to the singles by securing another title and one in men's doubles. Two more singles titles in 1960 and 1961, with men's doubles titles in both years with Chandrakant Deoras and a mixed doubles title in 1961 with Manda Kelkar, proved Natekar was a genius in all formats of badminton.

His focus on singles was unfettered, but he also enjoyed combining his grit with a partner. From 1962 to 1964, the country saw the rise of another prodigy, Suresh Goel. He took away three back-to-back titles in men's singles. Everyone was in awe of his style and game. A new name had emerged and a new wonder to witness. Natekar managed a doubles title in those years and one final singles title in 1965.

At the time, financial support from the government for sports was scarce. However, badminton fan Ramnarain Ruia – who was also the founder of the college Natekar studied at in Bombay – was keen on sending Natekar to the All-England Open Badminton Championship, which was by far the most prestigious competition of that era. The Maharashtra Badminton Association couldn't bear the costs, so Ruia established the 'Natekar Fund' to realise his dream.

Advertisements in newspapers led people to donation boxes set up during local matches. Natekar felt slightly embarrassed, but that was the only way. It was different from these days, to raise money at a time when sponsorships were non-existent. The required funds were raised, and Natekar made it to England. He put in a stunning performance to reach the quarterfinals but couldn't go further. He also participated in the US National Badminton Championships.

However, securing sponsorships remained a challenge, and Natekar could never compete abroad again. But it did not bother him as he was happy to play, no matter where. 'Natekar found it hard to cope with the western cold. If he knew this and had more experience of playing abroad, he would have landed in the country a little earlier, gotten himself acclimatised to the harsh cold and used his stroke-play and temperament to possibly win the title,' said Nadkarni confidently.

Natekar was a keen observer of the sport, and it took him little time to absorb what he had seen. He would follow each shot and the movement of the arms of seasoned masters and try to imitate them in his training sessions where he aimed for higher precision. With time, these shots and movements would only have a faint resemblance to the original, as Natekar would have rendered them in his own style.

Among these stalwarts was the Malaysian legend Wong Peng Soon. When Soon played a tournament in India, Natekar had the opportunity to learn the Malaysian's backhand technique. He also developed his footwork from watching players of high calibre. Natekar even impressed cricket great Sunil Gavaskar, who was a regular at the courts to play casually with friends. Gavaskar commented that Natekar's footwork made him seem gliding on the court. The two eventually developed respect and admiration for each other's abilities.

In an interview, Natekar said that he never liked being coached. 'I just played and learnt on my own,' he revealed. 'That's why I never looked at establishing an academy. My pleasure came from playing.' He did not lament that there were hardly any video recordings of his matches. Back then, they had a different style of training, which was not professional enough for international standards. A great player like Natekar hardly trained. He used to love playing badminton for hours but detested structured running and exercises or stretching. He had solid calf muscles because he spent that much time on the court. When you play so much, you go on your toes; you take the shuttle, push it back, come back, move forward, backwards and exercise all your muscles.

When asked how the sport has evolved, he said the gameplay is much faster now than in his time. He noted that a scientific approach was adopted by the players, who seemed to be more agile. 'We would have longer rallies,' he said, adding that he is delighted with the modern game. He also expressed his appreciation for the progress made by Indian women at the international level. 'They are quicker than the women players of my era,' he observed. 'I love the speed they display, reaching the net from the baseline in a flash.'

Natekar's badminton achievements have meant his skills at another racquet sport are often overlooked. Natekar loved tennis so much that before going for badminton training at Hindu Gymkhana, he would practise tennis for an hour daily. Badminton positively influenced tennis as his tennis shots resembled the flow of the arm one sees in badminton. In tennis, he would avoid shots like flicks and chose his badminton style to supersede, which many people found quite amusing, including himself.

His love for these two sports often overlapped, and thus, he could move on both courts with the same grace. It was hard to pick one for him. Then, to think of how he chose one over the other, it was a debate for sports scribes who suggested to his father that it was time for him to decide. That year, Natekar did well in badminton, and that's how the decision was made. Regrets never accompanied him on his journey.

'The three best male players India has produced are Natekar, Padukone and Pullela Gopi Chand. In my opinion and Natekar's contemporaries who have also watched Prakash and Gopi Chand play, unequivocally maintain that out of those Natekar was the best,' asserts Nadkarni.

He played in the national tennis tournament in 1951 and reached the final. In that match, he lost to Indian tennis legend Ramanathan Krishnan. Although Natekar eventually refocused on badminton, when his son Gaurav chose tennis over badminton, he did not try to change his mind. On reading about his son's wins in newspapers, Natekar's father wrote a letter when he was stationed in Baroda, reminding him of his priorities. It forms a fond memory for Natekar to have been reprimanded by his father on seeing a dismal performance in his studies. Who hasn't been through that?

Nandu Natekar was a generous person and polite to a fault. He passed away in 2021 at the age of eighty-eight.

3

Dinesh Khanna: Triumphs and Trials

DINESH KHANNA WAS BORN in 1943 into a royal family. His great-great-grandfather served in the cape of a Dewan, providing ministerial services to the throne. At that time, the throne seated a Sikh ruler, Maharaja Kharak Singh, son of Maharaja Ranjit Singh.

Fatehgarh Churian was where Khanna was to learn how to walk and cradle a racquet. It was home to between 5,000 and 7,000 people, but Khanna restricted himself from calling it a village. Its legacy should not be humbled.

The Sikh empire was to be usurped by the British Raj in 1849. And a few years later, Khanna's father began serving as the honorary magistrate in the British Empire. Post-partition, British India dissolved into India, Pakistan and East Bengal. And with that, the role that his father held was also suspended. He had to join the provisional civil services at Batala, now a city in Punjab. But soon, he was transferred to Amritsar, thirty kilometres away. The family shuttled between Fatehgarh Churian and Amritsar, where it owned a house. Khanna and his cousins had a lot of space outside the home, which they used for running around.

Khanna returned to Fatehgarh Churian while he was in seventh grade. Badminton had sparked his interest, owing to the game's straightforward nature, asking for just so much space that one could comfortably locate. Since it was a small town, it was not easy to find boys who would abandon sticks and stones, the mirthful ecstasy of running aimlessly or even cricket bats to be interested in a game of badminton. But Khanna was tactical, and the other boys were fit. That's all he wanted.

Khanna tempted local boys to play by promising cash prizes in small tournaments he arranged. The sweet smell of currency notes has always been a strong motivation. Knowing that the kids couldn't beat him, he made a simple rule: whoever could score three points against him would be rewarded with ₹ 2 – Khanna's pocket money for a week. He did not mind sacrificing the money as there was no other way to find a motivated opponent nearby.

He could not have spent that money elsewhere in that tiny town anyway. Sometimes, Khanna would raise the stakes and make the award more tangible – for example, a fountain pen, a luxury item for children in those days.

In 1956, when Khanna turned thirteen, he travelled back to Amritsar. He continued his schooling in the city, also colloquially known as Ambarsar. Once while playing with his cousins outside his home, Khanna learned of a shuttler named P. P. S. Chawla, whose uncle, P. S. Chawla, was an admired player in the 1950s. He used to train his nephew during the summer vacations.

P. P. S. Chawla and Khanna competed against each other in a badminton match. Khanna was confident but shaken when he lost 15–2. It was like waking up from an unforgettable nightmare, but it only made him more determined. It was the first time he had experienced such intense competition, and he eagerly awaited a stronger opponent to help him improve.

The Punjab Badminton Association in Amritsar had two attractive courts. His family had a contact in the association, and Khanna enrolled himself. He would take his bike and ride away to the courts, and the dust would settle only when he achieved his goal.

He was enamoured by the association's proposition for its youngsters – the best player in the state was rewarded with a monthly stipend of ₹200. The training back then involved mostly giving tips and some space to play.

He played in the Punjab state tournament. He reached the finals, where he again met his nemesis, P. P. S. Chawla. At least, that's what he considered him to be. 'This time, my score was much more respectable. But I did lose the match,' Khanna joked, even though it must have been traumatic back then, for he was reduced to being the runner-up. The rivalry was one-sided. Chawla even went on to play for the Indian team in its youth division during the early 1960s when the Indian side made a trip to Malaysia.

As Khanna recalled, Chawla was a respectable stroke player. The acknowledgement of his brilliance was accompanied by an admission of a physical condition he used to face, due to which he later switched to doubles. His strokes are still fresh in Khanna's memory and occupy an essential place in his repertoire of tales.

The same year, he appeared in his first junior nationals tournament, held at Panchkuian Road in Delhi and organised in a community centre. There was only one court for the junior and senior nationals, which took place simultaneously. Matches stretching late into the night were a common sight.

One such important event that distinguishes itself was when Natekar played against the captain of the Punjab team who was a reputed player. The match occurred in Delhi, in the unforgiving cold of a relentless December, at 3:30 a.m. Natekar was expected to win, which he did. But hailing from Mumbai, he needed to be tuned to bear the wintry chill of the north.

Returning to the 1956 nationals, Natekar played the final against T. N. Seth. In a contest of the champions, Natekar was world number 5, and T. N. Seth assumed the position of world number 8. These rankings reflected one's performance at the Thomas Cup, and India had fared well in the gathering. T. N. Seth didn't leave a single game for Natekar to anchor to, winning three games straight.

In the interstate team meet, Natekar had meted the same treatment to Seth. Revenge was served cold. It was a spectacle remembered by everyone who had the opportunity to witness it, and Khanna was one of them. The match was played on mosaic flooring, in which flattened pieces of stone or glass were put together to form glimmering designs. 'It is not safe to play on those, but that's how they played back then,' confirms Khanna. Wooden flooring was a luxury in Bombay's gymkhanas and some English clubs in north India.

The backhand stroke was not seen frequently. One would keep an eye on never letting the shuttle escape the ambit of their forehand. If they let it slip to their backhand, it was presumed the opponent would gain the confidence to snatch the ongoing point. Most of the seniors in Amritsar that Khanna saw never displayed adeptness in backhand play.

Watching T. N. Seth and Natekar, he understood the game could be played without succumbing to traditional weaknesses using both faces of a racquet and with comparable talent, if not equal. 'They both had fluent and powerful backhand strokes; I was enamoured and had decided to cultivate that in my game, too,' recalls Khanna.

Luckily, a friend in Bombay had a badminton manual with instructions and lessons on various strokes. It was authored by a badminton enthusiast, Ken Davidson. Khanna borrowed it and went straight to the page describing the backhand grip. Until then, he used to hold the racquet in his backhand just as he would hold it during a forehand stroke. Being a defensive player, knowing the backhand gave him the edge when his opponent sent an airstrike towards him. Every step mattered; saving a few gave him more stamina while waiting for the moment to score. 'I began to use my backhand for 70 per cent of the return shots. It became the pivot of my game,' said Khanna.

Gymkhanas and clubs in the larger cities often had 'markers', who would serve the shuttle to particular points on the court. It allowed the training players to practise specific strokes, such as a baseline smash or a concealed drop. But in Amritsar, players didn't have such a luxury. It made players like Khanna formidable stroke players who could improvise during a match. He said that curiosity led to a variety in his strokes because he had a propensity to test out different techniques.

In 1957, Khanna figured in the final of the Western India tournament held in Bombay. The tournament not only showcased the best talent from across the country but also had some international participants – such as the brothers Eddy and David Choong, who were among the top Malaysian badminton players. However, in the final, Khanna's nemesis Chawla was waiting for him. Khanna lost again. Khanna even went on to liken his strokes to those of Suresh Goel.

After returning to Amritsar, Khanna reached the final of the Punjab State Championship – where, once more, it was Chawla who lay in wait. Khanna struck hard this time and won the first game 18–17. It became clear that Chawla suffered from anxiety at crucial moments and was under pressure of his father's high expectations.

'He kept looking back at his father once the first game was taken away from him,' recalled Khanna. The second game became a cakewalk, with Khanna hardly conceding a point. He had resoundingly overcome one of the biggest challenges of his career till then. It was a welcome boost to his confidence and still quickens his heartbeat.

Badminton was a reasonably popular sport back then in the 1950s and 1960s. Cricket and hockey had a massive fan following, given how well Indians performed in these sports. Tennis, too, was closely followed by Indians, with Ramanathan Krishnan being one of the best players in the world. Twice, he climbed to the semifinals at Wimbledon.

India was doing reasonably well in athletics, with Milkha Singh having achieved feats that no other Indian had managed to acquire. Until the Partition, the National Championships saw six players from Punjab out of the eight quarterfinalists in men's singles. But post-1947, Punjab lost many of its players. Some prominent names from then were George Lewis, Nath and Devinder Mohan.

Nath was the runner-up in the 1947 All-England singles against Conny Jepsen. In 1949, during All-England, George Lewis was a match point up against Teik Hock Ooi of Malaysia in the quarterfinals. The linesman had a last-minute change of mind while trying to settle one of George's shots, but unfortunately, it was not in favour of George, so they called the shuttle out. It could have been the match-winning hit. From there, Teik Hock Ooi built a fabulous winning match.

If one thing Khanna's experience in badminton has proven to him, it is that the fierceness of competition sows the seeds of greatness. 'Look at any sport in the world, a country which breeds tough competitors progresses to produce some of the best athletes there will ever be.'

Khanna captured an international title before he secured a national one. He played in the Thomas Cup for the first time in 1963. He enjoyed a spell of rivalry with Suresh Goel, a genius at stroke-making and accuracy. He was well-versed in the art of shaking the confidence of his opponents. He was built slightly on the heavier side but had to train to keep his weight in check. 'At times, if Goel was late in reaching the net and the other player would be standing right next to it, Goel would deliver the shuttle in a way that it would just kiss the top of the net and topple over, all the while slyly whispering defeat to the helpless one,' said Khanna with eyes wide open.

The shuttle assumed a menacing character when it was with Goel. It knew the path it had to take, where to land and what damage it would do to the unwitting soul on the opposite side. His game contained a lot of deceptive manoeuvres ending with sharp shots. Khanna had previously lost to him twice in the singles final of junior nationals in 1957 and 1958. In 1957, Khanna lost the first game, but that did not bother him.

Goel's struggle with stamina meant Khanna could win the second one. He did and took the lead in the third. Then, all of a sudden, Goel found his second wind, leaving him stunned. It didn't take long for him to lose his lead and the game. Goel dealt a similar blow in the 1958 junior nationals where they again met in the final, turning Khanna's frenzy into a boiling pot.

After playing the nationals in 1960, Khanna began studying for an engineering degree in Chandigarh where there was no facility to practise shuttling. As a result, he did not participate in the nationals again till 1964. Only during trips to Amritsar on weekends would he get a little time on the court. In 1962, Goel won the singles national title against Dipu Ghosh. Even though Natekar was absent from the competition because of a leg injury, it was a noteworthy achievement, with Suresh becoming the youngest national champion at the age of nineteen.

Six months into the jubilation, trials for the Thomas Cup took place, and Goel and Khanna came face to face in the quarterfinals. Goel took the first game and expected to take home the match as well, but this time Khanna was not ready to let him off the hook so quickly. He defeated his opponent and quelled the jinx by winning the next two games.

'He probably took the match a little too lightly, and it was one of the rare occurrences when a national champion, that too a recent one, was not included in the national team. The Badminton Association of India wanted to prove that all were equal in its eyes and underscored the importance of trials,' reminisced Khanna. Goel was left in a daze with his exclusion from the team chosen for the Thomas Cup, a tournament of high repute occurring every three years, second only to the All-England Championships.

Indian participation in the All-England was infrequent, with players being sent only under exceptional circumstances. Using the same fury, he went on to win the coveted singles title in 1963 by weighing down on Natekar and again managed to secure the title the following year. Notably, their matches almost always entered the unsettling third game, giving all the excitement to their fans whose sighs carried an air of anxiety through the hall and, at times, a moment of relief.

Time went by, and history prepared itself for an unprecedented affair. Khanna graduated from college in 1965 and had more free time for badminton. The Asian Badminton Championship was approaching, and Khanna was called to a three-week training camp. Until then, his on-court activities were moulded by players who used to play at the state level. This was his first opportunity to train and play with the stars, including Natekar, Goel, Dipu Ghosh and Satish Bhatia.

Soon, the day arrived, and the championships began with a roar. Goel reached the semifinals by beating the top seed in the quarters. The match, according to Khanna, was the most fascinating one in the entire tournament. It was a close fight which went to the third game and jolted a lot of hearts into skipping beats by reaching a deuce at 13–13. It was customary to set the game to 18 after a deuce back then, but his opponent was so confident that he looked for a quick exit, setting the game at 15.

Goel stunned him by quickly snatching those two points. His opponent even tried some theatrics after that. 'He was a showman himself. He went up to the referee and tried to remind him that he had asked for a game of 18,' laughs Khanna. But the referee had decided, and Khanna was destined for a match with him again. Surprisingly, the semifinal was shorter, and Khanna finished it in the first two games. Khanna put it down to luck, being too humble about his achievement. 'I have been lucky against some of my rivals in deciding matches.'

But luck only takes one so far. What Khanna achieved requires determination, passion and hard work. His opponent in the final, Channarong Ratanaseangsuang of Thailand, was an abundantly experienced player with a ubiquitous presence in the international circuit. With considerably less experience, Khanna needed to learn how to take this fight. Khanna turned to renowned hockey player K. D. Singh to give him much-needed confidence. Singh – referred to as 'Babu' – was considered one of the best in the world at that time.

During a visit to Lucknow before the big tournament, Khanna had the chance to meet him. Babu wished him luck and, in turn, inspired him to take on any challenge. 'I thought to myself, if this fellow Indian could become one of the best in the world, then why couldn't I be at least the best in Asia,' Khanna reminisced. The twenty-two-year-old Khanna won 15–3, 15–11 and became the first Indian to win an Asian badminton title on 14 November 1965. The following year, he won the Commonwealth Games bronze medal.

He also accepted that Indians needed to see themselves as capable of outstanding sports achievements. This fact was indeed true back then. Singh's words were an essential motivation at a time when many Indian sportspeople believed that they were inferior to athletes from other parts of the world, at least in their physical capacity.

Khanna, famously called the 'Returning Machine', later contributed to the game by playing the role of a selector and also wrote extensively on badminton. He remained the brightest connection between the two eras of badminton that lit up India's reputation. He sometimes still wonders what a united Punjab team would have been like, untouched by the Partition, and only if British India had ceased to be reduced to its now smaller parts, since it was Lahore where all these top names used to have compulsory badminton bouts in the evening.

4

Trailblazers of the Past: Women's Badminton in the Mid-20th Century

WOMEN'S BADMINTON ATTRACTED A handful of participants in the first few years when Pearl Goss dominantly won the national singles title from 1936 to 1939. She also won in 1940 and then added her fifth individual crown nine years later. Her comeback was amazing, as she won her final titles thirteen years after having won the first. In 1942, the trio of Deodhar sisters took over and displayed their towering presence on the court.

Tara, Sunder and Suman were the daughters of the legendary Indian cricketer Professor D. B. Deodhar. One of the greatest batsmen in India's cricketing history, he played in an aggressive style. He captained the Maharashtra state team and moulded it into a formidable force in the Ranji Trophy. He played cricket through both world wars, and his achievements are well documented in the first-class cricket fraternity. The popular inter-zonal limited overs cricket tournament, Deodhar Trophy, is named after him.

Tara, Sunder and Suman were trailblazers in women's badminton. Sports was in the family, and it was hardly surprising that the sisters entered badminton and began dominating the national scene. The sisters won twenty-three national titles – singles, doubles and mixed doubles. Tara shone with her three successive wins in 1942, 1943 and 1944, while Sunder excelled with a triple crown in 1946. Later, Suman brought home the national singles title in 1951. Tara was good at studies too and finished a PhD in biochemistry from the US, where she met Rathalev and settled down with him in Denmark. For two years, in 1955 and 1957, Prema Prashar made a mark by claiming the singles.

The Apte sisters, Sarojini, Sunila and Sanjeevani, carved a niche with some dedicated performances in the 1960s. Sarojini was the eldest and the brightest, with six titles to her credit from 1962 to 1967. She made it to the finals in seventeen events. Her first four finals in singles resulted in consecutive losses to Meena before winning it in 1966 by overcoming her sister Sunila. Sarojini's maiden title happened because Meena had to give up playing due to a knee injury. Meena won the singles from 1959 to 1965 apart from three doubles and two mixed doubles titles.

Interestingly, Sarojini's triple crown in 1967 had come soon after her marriage. She teamed up with Dipu Ghosh in the mixed doubles to tame Sunila and Romen Ghosh. It was a rare occasion when two brothers and two sisters faced each other in doubles.

Sushila Rege Kapadia enjoyed a stellar career, winning eleven national titles from 1951 to 1963, with a triple crown in 1952 at Lucknow. She was a rage in the women's circuit because of her consistency. The Bombay-born Sushila won three singles (1952, 1953 and 1958), six doubles (1952, 1953, 1955, 1957, 1958, 1963) and two mixed doubles (1952 and 1957). She also earned a place in the Indian team when it went for its maiden Uber Cup appearance in 1956.

The sisters ruled the courts for a little more than a decade. Their retirement coincided with Natekar's arrival. During the years of Natekar's rivalry with T. N. Seth, when the latter was giving Natekar some trouble in singles, the nationals scene had a glimpse of a legend yet to come – Meena.

A deceptive player on the court and a loving heart away from it, Meena initially made her mark by winning women's and mixed doubles titles in 1956 and 1968, with J. Kour and Amrit Lal Diwan respectively. Her rise in singles, however, was a surprise to many. From 1959 to 1965, she seized seven consecutive titles in women's singles at the National Championships, showcasing her unmatched skill and determination. Her victories were unprecedented and unchallenged, marking a new era in Indian badminton.

Women's badminton had transformed into a more visible and independent form. The Deodhar sisters laid the foundation, and Meena carved out a special place. She proved that beauty and grace were not the only elements in women's badminton, but there was style, precision, an unforgiving spirit, and frequent displays of power. She was known in badminton circles for her hefty frame. Natekar recalls how the king of Thailand, Bhumibol Adulyadej, a badminton fan himself, was stumped to see her as part of the duo with Natekar to play the mixed doubles final of a tournament. And he was even more baffled to see her offset the plans her opponents had in mind.

Meena's frame never hindered her from achieving victories. According to old timers, her agility and speed on the court were a sight to behold. She was quick to judge and relentless in retrieving moves that seemed impossible to defend. There were matches when she would starve her opponents of points, demonstrating her unwavering determination and resilience.

Coming from Balrampur, a small town in Uttar Pradesh, Meena started her badminton career in Lucknow when her father was transferred. A master's degree in psychology was an added weapon in her arsenal. She could study a player's temperament and use it to her advantage to deal blows where they would hurt the most. Her dedication was unmissable.

T. N. Seth was appointed as the women's team coach in the late 1950s by the Uttar Pradesh Council of Sports, and he mentored her to become a formidable challenge on the court.

He would arrive at the practice nets with the only goal of developing each of her strengths. She would focus on improving her smashes, drops, tosses, or combinations. This helped her further enhance her stamina. When prodded about her frame and the supposedly contrasting ability on the court, she would credit God.

Meena primarily built her fitness through matches rather than rigorous exercises. During practice sessions, she would choose to stay on the court and play one or two more games than others.

Meena ruled the singles circuit till 1965 before developing issues with her knee. The year 1964 saw her winning the singles, doubles and mixed doubles. Her knee showed signs of letting her down for the first time in 1966 while playing singles in the Uber Cup that year. She attempted playing in the following year but had to pull back through the season again due to injury. Thinking of the toll it took on her knee, she stayed away from singles and concentrated on doubles. But the decision came at the cost of her satisfaction. It was like keeping a tigress in a reserve, and not in the jungles of Bengal, where it does what it does best.

Meena decided to compete in singles one last time. And thus, she went for the nationals of 1968. Ploughing through, Meena reached the semifinals and, by the skin of her teeth, managed to secure a place in the final. It showed the indomitable level at which she played badminton back then. But Meena felt the stress that her knee took. Just standing on the court, she watched the title slip away. She had to bid farewell. It was time. She had lost to Damayanti Tambay, a new name in the records that would highlight women's badminton for the next few years.

Another name that struck the chords of the experts was the demure Shobha. The quaint environs of Panchgani provided opportunities for Shobha to fall in love with badminton. The absence of good English medium schools in Kolhapur meant she had to move away from her hometown. It was a boarding school where all the games were compulsory.

The students played netball, throwball, hockey and football from January to May. The hockey field required the trainees to climb 100-odd stairs. The fitness lessons were learnt early. 'I was there for eleven years. The monsoon games were badminton and table tennis. The last quarter was athletics and tennikoit. It was a trip to Pune for a tournament that became the turning point in my life,' she recalled.

Badminton was an expensive game. 'One shuttle would cost ₹10, and it meant a lot in those times. There was nothing called sponsorship, and we had to buy used shuttles for cheap. The rent for a court was ₹1 per hour from 7 to 8 p.m. That was the prime time for us all, and we learned the game from the markers, really. The bonding between the players and the officials was strong. The competition among the players was healthy, and the respect was mutual.'

The best memories of her playing days was the simple life. 'Travelling by train was great fun. I barely slept during the journey, and it was a thrill to buy snacks at every station. They were great times with great challenges. I remember Manda Kelkar coming from a conservative family that wouldn't allow her to play in skirts. It took a lot of effort to convince her family. In some places, we faced trouble from the spectators, too.'

One of his friends advised Shobha's father to let her play badminton regularly. So, at the age of thirteen, she played a tournament in Nasik. She lost, but encouragement continued from her family. She won the national junior titles in 1960 and 1961 and chose badminton as a career, participating in all the tournaments in Bombay. The trophies adorned her drawing room, and she entered St Xavier's college as a promising player.

Manda Kelkar and Maureen Mathias were her partners in winning doubles. An Uber Cup appearance in 1960 enhanced her reputation. Being a stroke player, she was popular on the circuit. From 1968 to 1971, she ruled the badminton scene at the national level. Roman Ghosh was her partner in mixed doubles because he allowed Shobha to play at the back. 'I think we won eight titles together,' she remembered.

Shobha was Natekar's partner when he won his last title in 1971. 'I take great pride in the fact that I partnered with Natekar in his final appearance,' Shobha said. It was also the year that fetched her the prestigious Arjuna Award. She was the seventh badminton recipient of the Arjuna Award and the third after Meena and Damayanti Tambay.

Marriage in 1973 slowed down her career at the national level. She played a few local tournaments, won a few, and went for the nationals, where she faced Kanwal Thakar Singh. 'I led 8–0 but I was exhausted. I tried to get some rest by asking for a shuttle change, but I lost that game 8–11, and she beat me 11–0 in the third game. And that was the end of my competitive journey.'

Shobha follows badminton closely with praise for the modern generation, but she laments the lack of stroke-play, 'There is hardly anyone who flicks. I wish there was a player like Natekar. He would tire you and dictate. He was a great thinker and could read the breeze inside the hall. Remember, we hardly had any coaching those days and had to develop our game naturally. I would look at the footwork and strokes of my colleagues and opponents, think hard and execute.'

Born to a Maharashtrian mother (Shanta Devi) and a Telugu father (K. Radhakrishnan Moorthy), Shobha was a vital component of the badminton structure as she played all formats in singles and doubles. She made news by becoming the first to beat the legendary Meena. 'She said she was glad that I was the one who beat her,' said Shobha. The two remained friends after that.

According to Shobha, Meena was an outstanding player. 'She was fantastic. We had gone for the Uber Cup, and the crowd made fun of her because of her size. When she started playing, they were in a trance, admiring her movements. They were stunned into silence and ultimately gave her a standing ovation for her spirit.' Shobha was also fond of Sushila Rege, known for her high-quality serves. 'My neck would hurt waiting for the high-tossed serves to come down.'

Shobha believed none was better than Natekar for his 'perfect footwork'. She said, 'There was no need for him to run. Also, he hardly owned a racquet. He would casually borrow my racquet even for crucial matches. He was such a huge crowd-puller. At the CCI (Cricket Club of India), the queue for getting in would stretch to Marine Drive. Once at Guwahati, his appearance led to overcrowding of the temporary structure, which crashed, and the matches had to be called off.'

Shobha is delighted to see that badminton has grown. 'It was always popular, but there was hardly any money to be made in our time. Players took to the game because they loved it for fitness and recreation. It is a much-liked profession today, and I am so happy to see modern players living in style. Whenever there is a good contest, I get a call from Ami to switch on the TV. I love the aggression of our women players. There is much to take pride in what Sindhu and Saina have achieved. Even the Chinese dread Sindhu. That is unthinkable for those who know the dominance of the Chinese.'

Shobha coached the juniors at the CCI along with Hufrish Nariman in the 1990s before deciding to spend time with her grandchildren. Occasionally, she is spotted among the spectators at local tournaments in Mumbai.

5

Damayanti Tambay: Grace on the Court

At the war widows Association in south Delhi, she devotes time to a cause dear to her. Damayanti Subedar-Tambay is a war widow. Her marriage was just one year old when her husband, Flt Lt Vijay Tambay, went missing in the India–Pakistan war in 1971. She was convinced that he was being held in a Pakistani jail despite his body never being recovered. Damayanti firmly believed that her hero would return one day. She moved heaven and earth and made innumerable petitions to various authorities, but her efforts ran into an impregnable wall.

'I got married in 1970,' she reflected on her happy days. 'We were in Ambala, which had no courts. I had to travel to Allahabad to play badminton, and Vijay was very keen on my career. He wanted me to win one more title with Tambay as my surname. I won the title for him in Hyderabad. Sadly, they did not send the team for the Commonwealth Games even though I was in the camp for four months. I got the Arjuna Award the same year. After I lost him in the war, I tried to come to terms with life. JNU had this post, and I got the job. I moved to Delhi in 1972.'

Damayanti had a wonderful childhood. Among four siblings, she was the third. She remembers training at the Mayo Hall Sports Complex and imbibing qualities to pursue a career in sports from her parents – her father,

Sharad Kumar, was a lawyer, and her mother, Vijayalakshmi, was a teacher from Indore. Incidentally, she is a first cousin of Indian cricketer Rahul Dravid. 'I have never met Rahul,' she pointed out. Her best memories are of learning the game from Suresh Goel, one of the greatest players in India's badminton history.

It was a privilege few would have dreamt of. Goel would reach her home at dawn and ring the bell to wake Damayanti. She had no option but to pick up her racquet and pillion ride to the training spot. 'There was this fear that I may fall off because I would be too sleepy,' she laughed. But she had to accompany Goel, who was considered an incredible talent in Allahabad.

Goel, the idol she admired, ignited her love for badminton. Damayanti was adept at combining her school and the time spent in badminton. A badminton career was unimaginable until she discovered her passion for sports.

There was support from home since her brother, too, liked badminton. The first time she accompanied him to a selection camp, her brother's name appeared in the newspaper. 'My name was missing. I was ten. I just sat there and continued in the camp. I learned the basics of backhand and forehand. You don't have to be strong in badminton to play the big shots. It was all timing and accuracy. That camp helped me. I was eleven when I first went out to play out of town (at Faizabad). The junior tournament was played with the boys because I was the only girl. There was a team from Lucknow. One Mrs Kapoor was there, and she took me as a partner. She told me to cover the net, and we won the doubles title. She did everything.'

Damayanti made no secret that she was an average academic student. 'I did my class ten at the age of twelve. At seventeen, I was doing my first year in college when I went for the All-England. Today, the kids are brighter. I wish I were brighter,' Damayanti remembered.

How does she look at her story? 'My story. What is my story?' she quipped. 'My life may be a story for you, but not for me. For me, it is my life. How can I start speaking about myself? From when? From when I became conscious of things around me, or from when I stopped playing badminton?'

Damayanti had a badminton background. Her parents played badminton every evening at a club. Her mother was good at badminton and table tennis. 'She played in a saree.' Damayanti smiled.

Sport was important then, too. There were no distractions, and kids were kept busy on the sporting field. Coaching was decent at the district level. Badminton attracted many aspirants. 'A good thing is that badminton is an indoor game. Weather conditions don't affect badminton. It has the advantage of being played round the year. It gives you happiness because you get a sense of accomplishment. It is a simple game for beginners, but later, it becomes as tough as any other sport.'

Playing badminton was fun, but studying was equally important. 'In the off-season, we used to store the racquets in a wooden frame, but later we switched to steel frames which we screwed onto all four sides. We had to be careful with our racquets because we couldn't afford to buy new ones.' Over time, there have been changes in the sport's gear and clothing, but the game's dimensions have remained the same.

Goel was a significant influence on Damayanti. He helped her into competitive badminton, too. 'He was five years older than me. To see his game was divine. There was nothing that he did not have. Not one stroke that he lacked. Beautiful backhand and overhead. He never appeared to be making an effort, touch, flicks, or deception in his game. I learnt it from him by watching him. He was so smooth on the court that he never had an injury. He was music on the court. I wish I could describe him better. I was blessed to have played along with him and watched him in action. We learnt from watching mostly. There was no coach as such.'

Shirish Nadkarni reiterates words of Damayanti: 'If you want a stroke for stroke comparison, then Goel was a better stroke-maker than even Natekar. His style effused enough magic to captivate the best of the best from the world of badminton.'

Those were times of simplicity. Competition was welcome but not with an attitude of 'win at all costs'. You had to have the strength to last the match. So, fitness was necessary. 'Fitness? I had yet to learn. No one told us. I saw Goel running and skipping. I also did. Before dinner, I used to skip, bend, and stretch. How else do you strengthen your stomach muscles?'

Damayanti pointed out that lack of overseas exposure was a valid factor. 'I played just one All-England, one Uber Cup, and made one trip to East Africa. Things have changed. Today, they will go out twice a month. I had a chance when Judy (Hashman) invited me, but who would pay for the tickets? We had no sponsors. No one gave us money. Look at the gear we had. I had a pair of Dunlop shoes and two racquets. Once, I lost my bag and the racquets. Then someone gave me two pairs of racquets, one pair of skirts, two T-shirts and one jersey – no foreign stuff. My shoes were Bata shoes and no branded racquets. Then came Slazenger. We would get two racquets every month.'

She fondly recalled the trip to England: 'The All-England Championship was mind-blowing. It was an unforgettable experience. The hall was huge, and there was a drift. That was a challenge. Service was a huge challenge. My first exposure became the last. The setting in England was so different.

Within the limitations and opportunities, we did what we could. I am grateful for whatever I got.'

Damayanti confessed she never thought playing badminton was easy. 'You would have played six matches to figure in the final. It was not easy because if you said that, you undermined the opposition. I looked to give my best that day. Fifty years have passed, and I remember my game and the journey well. My biggest asset was my backhand. I never faulted on my backhand.'

Opponents were in awe of Damayanti, for she could hit a smash on the backhand. 'They could not attack my backhand. And, of course, the flicks. I won many crucial matches on my backhand. I am trying to figure out how I managed that. I didn't choose the backhand over the forehand. Why should I convert? Why discard my strong area? For me, it saved time. It came naturally. I don't know when I imbibed it. I feel that sometimes I knew a lot of finer points about the game, which I should have imparted. I gave up playing for personal reasons. I wish I could have passed it on.'

Damayanti spoke from her heart at the mention of Judy Hashman. 'Judy was an amazing player with seventeen All-England titles, eighteen to her father, and six to her sister, making it a total of forty-one world titles in one house. Judy and I lost touch for eighteen years, but in 1984, while I was with JNU, I decided to watch the Olympics in Los Angeles, where I met her. I stayed with her for some time. In 1985, she was invited to Lucknow for two months to train kids.'

Damayanti's time with Judy was a lesson in coaching. 'We talked about badminton whenever we met. Her teachings were applicable even in normal life. How do you deal with life?'

The sessions in Lucknow were held on two courts, and Judy never took her eyes off. She would stand and keep an eye on the two courts. 'What discipline and dedication! No one has come close to her achievements on the court. My God, All-England was bigger than the World Championships because it had a larger participation of players. She loved me to be attached to her during the coaching. It was an education. She would start the training at 10–all, creating the pressure. It was an amazing style of teaching. Start with the 10 – love deficit and challenge yourself to make the points to win.'

Damayanti insisted none taught better than Judy. 'Dealing with pressure was what she taught so well, but she also taught me how to concentrate on my mental fitness. You can develop physical attributes by running and exercising, but she taught mental toughness. She would ask the trainee to tackle three shuttles. I remember Yonex bringing about a hundred special racquets to celebrate Judy and her father's feats. I still have one of those racquets. Her methods were so inventive and also focused on accuracy. Look at her dedication to badminton. She is my inspiration.'

Judy, she said with a smile, is a dear friend. 'Imagine, she first won the All-England title when she was seventeen and the last one at thirty-one, when she was a mother. I visit her every year. Also, how many can boast of having the All-England gold medal? I have it in my house. Saina and Sindhu are doing so well but don't have the medal I have in my collection. Judy came to India in 1966 and gave me that year's medal.'

Damayanti won her junior titles in 1962 and 1963 and senior crowns in 1968, 1969 and 1970. The one in 1968 against Meena, and subsequent ones against Shobha. 'Meena had won seven consecutive titles. Her all-round game was perfect. Her weight misled you into believing that she was slow. She trained very hard, and she was very accurate. She was a role model for most of us. Meena was a great player.'

Damayanti reflected on those glorious days when the sport was not so commercial. 'Our approach was simple. If you win, feel happy. If you lose, move on – honestly, there was no fixed strategy. I had confidence in my game. Today, I see these players look at their coach every time they concede a point. I don't understand this. What about using their brain? I would stop this way of coaching.'

The challenges in modern badminton compel the players to think differently. 'You are not getting angles these days. Toss, drop, not there. There is more fitness and staying power. We did not have that fitness. I can say the strokes are limited. Angles are the most critical aspect of badminton. Sindhu takes offence in hand and sometimes appears to be a slow-paced player. Speed of your legs and strokes must match.'

The game has also changed for some off-the-field demands. 'The game changed because there is money. I understand you must make the game television friendly to attract sponsorship. Make it fast. What more can you get into the game? The scoring system has changed. The game's sustainability depends on TV and sponsorship. They look at viewership. Now, you are reaching out to the young generation.'

Damayant's niece, Mekhla Subedar, was a national champion in squash for four years. A cousin, Kritika, was a chess champion for two years. She is proud of her family. After retirement, Damayanti devoted time to badminton as a commentator for Doordarshan and ESPN. 'There are no bad things about badminton. I love the game and the players.'

Among her prized possessions is this message from her loving husband:

Dearest Damayanti,

Whenever you see this photograph, our hearts will get together, regardless of the distance between us – whether I am flying or you are thrashing your opponent 11–0 on the badminton court.

Your loving husband,
Vijay.
28th October 1970

She loves badminton and the thought that Vijay will return one day. The story of Damayanti is that of a champion whose career was curtailed well before its time.

6

Arif Saab: Crafting Legends Through Coaching

THE HALL AT THE Lal Bahadur Stadium, Fateh Maidan is brimming with activity. The sound of squeaking shoes is a pleasant reminder that the courts are in use, as Syed Mohammed Arif keeps an eye on the trainees, sitting on a chair from his corner. It is a routine he has followed for nearly four decades. Arif Saab, as he is popularly known, is an institution in himself.

'Close to 350 champions at all levels have emerged from these very courts,' Arif states. His mind wanders into the past, but his eyes are in the present, taking in every inch of the courts. His hawk-like observations keep the trainees on their toes.

'Can you admit my daughter to your academy?' a mother pleads. Arif smiles, pats the little girl on her head, and clarifies, 'She can come, but not at the cost of studies. She will have to attend all her classes at school without being distracted by these courts. Once I assess her talent, we shall see how far she can continue her love for badminton.'

The Fateh Maiden is a landmark venue famous for staging cricket matches, both domestic and international. It sits in the centre of the city and welcomes aspirants from all walks of life. Arif has seen the city grow from a laid-back populace to a fast-moving metro where everyone is engaged in a race to excel.

Hyderabad has always been one of the major badminton centres in India, even when the current facilities – now available to thousands of young shuttlers – were not there.

'The fact that some of the top BAI officials hailed from Hyderabad and Vijayawada only helped the cause of the local players by way of several national and international tournaments. For instance, a legend like Liem Swie King of Indonesia, played at Fateh Maidan Indoor Stadium,' said V. V. Subrahmanyam.

'The success stories of players like Manoj Kumar, Praveen Kumar and Vijay Raghavan, to name a few, on the national scene were an inspiration for someone like Gopi Chand. One remembers the packed Fateh Maidan Indoor Stadium when the senior nationals were held for one last time in 1991, lustily cheering the players. Fateh Maidan was the only major centre to train these young talents, with some others like Railway Institute's indoor stadium IRISET coming up later,' remembered Subrahmanyam.

One of the main reasons for the emergence of so many badminton players is the structure of domestic tournaments across all age groups in Andhra Pradesh and Telangana. There has always been a calendar for all age groups featuring inter-district tournaments from which young talent emerged.

'Whatever results we have in badminton is thanks to the commitment and sincerity of badminton officials over the years and with the kind of support the sport received from the state governments over the years,' stressed Subrahmanyam.

Arif's philosophy may not match the pace of today's youth, but he remains firm in his principles at any stage. Their dedication is drawn from his service to badminton. He is selfless and committed to producing responsible citizens and, of course, champions. Gopi Chand, Saina, and Sindhu are some of the stars who have benefited from his early lessons in the basics of the game.

'I still insist on the basics. Without a proper foundation, the building can't stay stable,' Arif beckons a trainee. 'Your footwork is not up to the mark today. Take a break.' Arif encourages innovations on the court and does not like the trainee fumbling.

These courts opened around 1970 when Hyderabad hosted the national championships. They were not even covered. 'A very peculiar thing about that time was that all this roof was a single piece. We have practised in a single hall – pathetic conditions all our lives. There was no concept of training earlier, and there was no space to tell the truth,' he remembers.

Arif found the facilities challenging to keep the training going. 'I used to get six shuttles a day for seventy-five trainees. I remember Skylark shuttles. I would tell them not to smash. Just try the drop shot. I would borrow used shuttles from other academies.'

When Arif assumed charge, most of the senior players were already on the downhill. 'I caught hold of a new batch. I used to run with them earlier in the morning, from 5:30 in the summer to 6 o'clock in the winter. We used to start the training with small children at that time. And I found that within a year, they had started performing.'

Arif began his coaching career in 1978 in Jammu and Kashmir. It took him four years to develop a system of training with regularity. He has vivid memories of those tough years. 'I would come and just sit in the chair for three hours because they did not have a training system. I coaxed one boy to come. Slowly, the number grew, and I put them through the rigours of coaching. I put a system in place, and it slowly started showing results. The poor maintenance of your fitness level causes sports disorders in India. To reach your goal, you must overcome the obstacles within yourself. You get tired, and you have to fight against yourself. That's when you improve.'

The titles grew in different age groups and categories, like men, women, singles, doubles, junior singles, doubles, and sub-junior singles, combining the girls with the boys. 'More than 230 titles and over 330 players who have played for the country began their careers from these courts. Manoj and Praveen were the first to win titles in the USSR in 1987. They started the trend.'

He is clear on one count. 'You may have the talent, but nothing without the fitness.' He implores the students to set a target because they are trying to win against the opponents by raising their level. Gopi Chand and Saina have come through this system and these courts. They showed the attitude to become champions.

'Let me tell you, none of my students here were second class. Gopi was in the same category. He opted for badminton over his studies. You can only be good at sports with brains. I left the choice to him. I told him not to take up tough subjects at school. He chose commerce. I am happy he made the right decision at the right time. I remember a jeweller sponsoring him – five Yonex racquets and three international tournaments – when I wanted him to play ten to twelve tournaments.' Gopi participated in the German League and beat some of their best players.

Arif has seen the growth of badminton in India – from the grassroots to the international stage – in a glorious career as a coach. Not the one to clamour for rewards and recognition, he has remained grounded in his approach to the job, always consumed in his work. He is just the person to guide a youngster who may have been trying his best to pick up the nuances of the game.

He is able to read a trainee well. 'An innate quality' he claims to have developed through his interactions with hundreds of trainees. 'I work on motor abilities. Two types of age categories – biological age, the real age when they were born, and the training age.'

Training age takes a realistic stock of the player's capacity after a couple of years to assess the resistance power. Careful monitoring is needed due to the technical nature of the exercises; in the initial stages, specific exercises may not be suitable for young trainees and should not be prescribed to them.

Arif knew India had the talent. After finishing his NIS (National Institute of Sports) course, he studied hard to find the fundamental weaknesses and strengths of the Indian players. How could they be made more successful? Arif travelled to watch the Chinese, Indonesians, Koreans, Malaysians to understand their style and tactics and concluded that fitness gave them the advantage.

'And it was no secret that their performances came on the strength of their exceptional levels of fitness and well-developed motor abilities.' Arif was among the early coaches who realised that the Indian players had a good degree of stroke production, and their deception on the court was second to none. 'We produce some of the best stroke players in the world.'

The challenge, if one can call it that, for the coaches comes from the trainees' parents. Arif firmly believes that parents should 'encourage and not interfere' with their kids' progress. 'It is fine to be enthusiastic, but they should draw a line. These days, there is more involvement from the parents. One parent once asked me if I always talk about the kids, but what about the motivation of the parents? I asked him, 'Do you want your child to be a doctor or an engineer, and did the child become one in three months? You have to give the coach and your child time to develop.'

The trainees need to develop their mind and body to achieve their goals. They can improve their mental abilities but must also work hard on their physical abilities. Training hard can bring injuries. 'I can't have my trainee be a bundle of injuries.' Arif understands the trainee's capacity and avoids pushing too hard at a young age to prevent career-threatening injuries.

Modern badminton requires muscle development to achieve one's maximum potential. After puberty, an individual's muscles develop naturally based on bone structure. 'The process is entirely based on scientific principles and cannot be rushed. It is essential to have patience and understand that muscle development takes time. It typically takes three to four years at the junior level to see noticeable progress and another eight to ten years at the international level.'

Do individuals fight personal battles? For example, Sindhu? 'Most of them are the same when they come to me. As they develop and train, they show more enthusiasm and don't accept defeats. It is a good sign if they weep. It's a good sign if they don't accept defeats. That is a good attitude. I remember Sindhu was nine when she came to me. Her readiness to work was amazing. She never shunned practice sessions. She adapted quickly. She wanted to be No. 1, and Sindhu had been giving such vibes since childhood. I worked for four years on her endurance and agility on the court. Her basics are strong, and Gopi Chand expertly shaped her.'

Has he ever chided Sindhu or Saina? 'I am never tough. In my fifty years of coaching, I was late only twice. Once by half a minute and once by a minute. I was afraid of coming late. What would my students think of me? Sindhu was always on time. She was calm and composed. She is a national treasure. My trainees developed discipline that helped them in life. I am proud of that.'

Comparing Saina and Sindhu, Arif said the former is a retriever. 'Sindhu is an attacker. Retrieving needs a lot of strength. Saina jumps and attacks on the forehand. She gets behind the shuttle. Sindhu has always wanted to be an attacking player, and we have worked on her speed and jump. I also taught her to create an opening. She improved her net play and dribbling with a sound base. In later years, she lost many a rally, but she overcame those issues by developing her overall game.'

Players have different qualities – footwork, strong and supple wrist, strong shoulders. Some move slowly on the court. What are the three most important in that order? Arif enlightens, 'Badminton is one of the toughest games. Take running. It can be cyclic. Some games require a sideward fake, like basketball. In badminton, we have forward, backward and sideward. No other game has such a variety of movements. Forward and backwards make badminton very challenging. The abdomen and back have to be very strong. Your explosive jumps, endurance, speed, flexibility, execution of shots, shoulders, back, heart and lungs contribute to your game. It can be a fascinating study because there are ten things the player is thinking about each shot. A badminton player is an epitome of fitness at all times.'

Arif is best qualified to analyse the game's evolution, having watched Ami, Madhumita, Manjusha and Aparna. Sindhu's contribution to popularising the game has been immense, and Arif agreed wholeheartedly. 'Earlier, the game was based on strokes. Let me give you an example. Meena was heavy, and people would mock her. At her last camp, she had come for the Uber Cup; she played some lovely tosses. She realised the game had changed and acknowledged the speed. Women would smash very little, maybe five times. Today, they are smashing fifty times in a match. Prakash (Padukone) would mesmerise his opponents with deception and not by smashing. Indians have very supple wrists and must concentrate on this aspect. Few international players have the deception that the Indians have.'

Can he pick one modern player as a complete player? 'No one can beat Padukone. No one. He was a complete player. In women, Sindhu, yes, but the most talented I have come across is Jwala Gutta. In the late 90s, she showed exceptional talent. Jwala was a fantastic player on the court, but off the court, she would shirk. I remember Kanwal. She attended some fifteen camps with me, and I found her one of the most robust players ever. She was the first player to beat Ami.'

Did he foresee Modi beating Padukone? 'I had said Prakash was not the same after going to Morten Frost as a sparring partner. At Vijayawada (National Championships), his match had to be postponed from morning to afternoon. His movements were not the same. Modi was a highly talented player, and I was not surprised because Prakash had lost touch with the shuttle brand used in India.'

Rajeev Bagga beating Padukone? 'A lot of it had to do with the quality of the shuttle. Prakash was right in pointing this out. He lost to Bagga, and the federation decided to change the shuttle brand.'

Arif can't miss a session at the stadium. Travelling from his home in the old city to Fateh Maidan has been an inseparable part of his life. 'My house is a hundred years old. My mother lived for over a hundred years. I am eighty. In fact, if I don't come to the stadium, my wife will come up with a hundred questions.' Arif is rightly called the grand old man of Indian badminton and is a decorated coach.

7

Prakash Padukone: The Icon

Prakash Padukone is synonymous with Indian badminton. His is a story of perseverance that has been told and retold over the last four decades. His exceptional talent, remarkable consistency, and unwavering humility has inspired generations of badminton enthusiasts.

A badminton fan in India could not have asked for a more intense confrontation than Syed Modi taking on Padukone. Experts believe it was the best phase of Indian badminton in the modern era as the two demonstrated great respect for each other on the court. There was no animosity between them, and the audience benefited from their splendid spirit.

For those who watched them regularly and from close quarters, what stood out was the fact that there were no easy points to gain. Long rallies were the standard feature during their matches, with a sense of accomplishment upon clinching the contest. However, Modi's rise coincided with Padukone's decline.

The 1980 All-England Championship was a landmark moment in Indian badminton when Padukone tamed Liem Swie King in straight games to win a title no Indian had. Shirish Nadkarni was among the privileged in the audience and raved about Padukone's achievement in his book *Courting Success*.

'A long rally, a late flick of the wrist from the twenty-four-year-old Indian to send the bird over his rival's head, and a despairing Swie King return into the net – and King Prakash had conquered the badminton world,' wrote Nadkarni. Padukone won 15–3, 15–10, and Indian badminton took a giant leap. Padukone obliged Nadkarni's request for the T-shirt with which he had played the final. The maestro now wants the T-shirt back for his museum which he plans to set up at the Padukone–Dravid Centre for Sports Excellence. Nadkarni is happy to part with the prized souvenir, 'If you manage to start such a museum, then in the national interest, I will be more than willing to return it.'

Those were days when sponsorship was meagre in terms of money. Players were happy to acquire racquets free of cost, and some travel privileges were welcome too. In Padukone's case, support came from various quarters, and he made the most of it. It had the good wishes of the nation, which had long craved for champions.

Padukone's conquest in London came three years before Kapil Dev's team was to make cricket history at Lord's. He had drawn inspiration from the 1975 hockey World Cup win at Kuala Lumpur and motivated a generation of youngsters to think big.

The All-England title completed Padukone's sensational run, which saw him claim the Danish Open and Swedish Open. He was in the form of his life and translated it into a treasured phase on the court. There was unprecedented joy in his triumph, and the cavalcade in Bombay only underlined the significance attached to Padukone landing on Indian soil after a trophy won overseas.

Former India star Khanna called Padukone's win a 'coup' in his column in *Sportstar*. For someone who would get to play merely two or three tournaments annually in his initial years, Padukone's feats at the international level were admirable. In 1973, Padukone made his debut appearance in the All-England Championship. However, he missed the next three years, which were critical years of his career. Despite this setback, he proved his talent and resilience by reaching the quarterfinals in 1973.

As his former doubles partner Leroy recalled, 'Prakash mastered strokes but didn't know how he could control the net. He could keep the shuttle close to the net. When Prakash swung the racquet and made contact with the shuttle, it would fall within an inch of the baseline. I have made him demonstrate it to my students. I have witnessed someone like Zhao Jianhua dancing to his tune; he didn't know whether to go back or front. He probably was practising those by himself. He invented ways to master strokes.' It was clear that Padukone followed the saying, 'necessity is the mother of invention'.

Initially, Padukone was inclined to play other sports like cricket, table tennis and basketball. However, the 1970 national junior championships clinched his interest in badminton. He was fifteen and had to decide. Badminton it was.

'It is amazing how Prakash hailed from Karnataka, a state that had very few badminton players at the time. Despite no proper coaching or guidance, he went on to win many titles and inspire the entire nation,' said Uday Pawar, a four-time men's doubles national champion.

There have been many inspiring stories in Indian sports, but few match Padukone's passion. He had no access to proper training facilities and had to practise in a wedding hall. During the wedding season, badminton would take a back seat. In an interview, he revealed that he did not care about the lack of facilities but made good use of whatever was available.

Padukone's influence extended beyond the badminton court. His dedication and discipline were emulated by athletes across India. His admirers included the elite, with Sunil Gavaskar, one of the greatest cricketers of all time, expressing his admiration for Padukone. His legacy lives on in the hearts of those he inspired.

Loved by his contemporaries, Padukone had great praise for his opponents, too. He had said in an interview that Rudy Hartono, the legend from Indonesia, had the greatest influence on his game. Padukone watched the training that Hartono brought to his preparation, which changed his attitude.

'Prakash used to wait outside Rudy's room early in the morning to follow him to the practice sessions. By scrutinising each move on the court, Prakash learnt his key badminton lessons by observing. He was an equally good doubles player, and the lessons I learned by being his partner have helped me in coaching Chirag (Shetty),' recalled Pawar.

In the opinion of former player turned scribe Sanjay Sharma, 'Prakash was the most outstanding player in both national and international circuits. He could carry the burden adeptly. He was the only player with a strong backhand and forehand, had an immaculate balance on the court and was a helpful character. With his deception, he could fox players like Morten Frost and Han Jian.'

The fact that Padukone never made any demands from the authorities spoke for his focus on what he had to do. He would request support to facilitate his participation in tournaments overseas. There was a time when he craved competition. At home, there was hardly any resistance to his dominance. He won the national senior title along with the junior crown in the same year – 1972. He reigned supreme for eight years until Modi stopped his brilliant run in 1980.

Padukone wanted good conditions and money for the players. The trio of Sri Ram Chadha, Fazil Ahmad and Ahmed Hussain was in control of the Badminton Association of India. They were running the federation and jockeying the positions between them. One became the president, the other secretary, and the third became treasurer. They used to swap positions. They held the badminton community to ransom, literally. 'Padukone looked to start a rival association and was getting quite successful at it. However, when he tried to get an affiliation with the International Badminton Federation, which is now BWF or Badminton World Federation, he could not succeed because these people had formed a caucus with the top people in the IBF,' recalled Nadkarni.

Padukone faced a little challenge on his home court during his maiden national title tournament. The tournament was held in February 1972 instead of December 1971 due to the war against Pakistan. In a thrilling match held in Madras against Devinder Ahuja, Padukone lost the first game 8–15 but quickly rebounded by winning the next game 15–3. Padukone's exceptional temperament in the final game led him to win 18–17.

For Padukone, it was a momentous day. He began with a semifinal win against Sanjay Sharma in the juniors, beat Ahuja for the senior title, and less than an hour later tamed Hanumantha Rao of Andhra 15–11, 15–10 in the junior final. It proved his precocious talent and physical energy to overcome stiff opposition at a young age.

It was a sensational win for a player who had started his career at the state level in 1962 as a sub-junior, losing in the first round. Two years later, he won the state championship. Despite losing his first-ever competitive match in a local tournament, he was rewarded with the 'best loser' trophy to console him.

His contemporaries respected Padukone's progress at the international level. He added titles at regular intervals, beginning with the men's team bronze medal at the 1974 Asian Games in Tehran. Two years later, he won the individual bronze in the Asian Championships at Hyderabad and the prestigious gold at the 1978 Commonwealth Games in Edmonton.

The World Cup bronze at Kyoto in 1980 – when he was ranked world number 1 – was a precursor to the 1981 gold at Kuala Lumpur in the World Cup. He was now ready for the All-England crown.

In 1983, he collected the bronze at the World Championships in Copenhagen. In the same year, he signed off with the Asian Championship silver in the men's team. His first silver medal came at the 1988 US Open in the doubles with Liem Swie King.

But Padukone was gradually falling back on the big stage. Titles were elusive. At home, Modi was making rapid strides. It was time for Padukone to take the complex but essential call on his love for the game. The defeat at the hands of Rajeev Bagga at the Jammu nationals in 1991 called the curtains on his illustrious career.

Born on 10 June 1955, Padukone, as acknowledged by many in the badminton fraternity, was blessed with God-gifted talent. He had an incredible eye for the shuttle. He could retrieve the shuttle from the most challenging positions and place it in the corners beyond the opponent. There was a certain precision about his game. Youngsters would watch his practice sessions for hours. The phrase 'education in discipline' was used to describe it. It was a reflection of his character. He was never the one to hurt anyone – a smiling assassin, one could say.

His grandfather, Annoji Rao Padukone, had settled in Bangalore from a village, and he would organise tennis tournaments. His father, Ramesh, had interest in cricket and hockey but promoted badminton on a big scale.

Kiran Kaushik, a childhood friend of Padukone, paints a compelling picture of the champion shuttler. 'His father was very disciplined. The quality was inherited by Prakash. Initially, Prakash played cricket and basketball.

He was an opening batsman, and I am sure he would have become a decent cricketer, but his love for badminton was greater. One good thing was that he was passionate about badminton, but not at the cost of his studies. It was clear that education was an important part of his growing up years,' Kaushik recalled.

Padukone joined the Union Bank as a probationary officer, and the Swedish Open earned him a prize of ₹ 3,301 and a promotion to a Grade 1 Officer. 'He was sincere with his job. He had permission to go to practice at 3 p.m., but he would work until 5 p.m. and wait for me to finish, and then we would train together. He never neglected his office work. Had he continued to work with the bank (he turned professional after winning the All-England), I am sure Prakash would have risen to the rank of managing director of the bank,' said Kaushik. The bank later sponsored his training in Indonesia, which Padukone was grateful for and said was the turning point of his career.

Padukone, who won the national title nine times, was a gifted and hard-working player. He was not known to complain about the facilities. He was comfortable even with a small hall and adapted to the larger ones when he travelled overseas. 'Amazing how he took things in his stride,' Kaushik noted.

A once-in-a-generation player, Padukone would often train against two opponents on the other side of the net. 'So many times, two of us would play against him, and he would win,' Kaushik recalled. He had started as a defensive player but added some aggression after watching the Chinese in action at the 1974 Asian Games.

Simplicity was Padukone's forte. His contemporaries say they never saw Padukone lose his cool. He always kept his problems to himself – no ill feelings towards anyone. 'But on the court, he showed no mercy. He was a very gracious person. He could have smashed his opponents at zero, but he would give away at least a point. He was polite and a very down-to-earth person. I have seen him sleep on the floor and eat whatever was served at camps and during tournament. I can tell you he loves food and is a voracious eater. He has been so since I have known him for more than fifty years,' raved Kaushik, who won the national doubles title partnering Padukone in 1979.

The half-court smash, delivered with a deceptive angle, helped Padukone overcome many a strong opponent. He mastered it through hard practice and used it at the right time to clinch a rally. His fans marvelled that he moved so gracefully on the court without making a sound. 'It was as if you were playing against a ghost because he hardly made any sound with his quick movements on the court. A stealth bomber he was,' smiled Kaushik.

Rudy Hartono, the Indonesian terminator, had already conquered the hearts of many internationally. Before, no one had seen his game in full, perhaps only brief glimpses of his image here and there. He was both swift and destructive in his prime.

Players who had the opportunity to witness his conquests were in awe of his menacing power to damage the temperament that his opponent carried with care to the court. His beefy strength and stamina of a horse had to have a story, and Padukone was hellbent on satisfying his curiosity to know the causes that could shape such physicality.

Hartono challenged the game style and dominated the courts worldwide with the beauty of a deceptive knock or the occasional drop. Until now, there used to be stillness in the game. But he needed more patience for long rallies. He would charge the shuttle like a bull when it began its flight from the other end to settle it on the ground.

He was the youngest All-England champion, only seventeen in 1968, and – if there was any way he could make the record grander – he won it in his first attempt.

All-England Championship is widely considered the most prestigious badminton tournament in the world. India was already a testament to Hartono's crushing show when he used to visit. With few international tournaments occurring, top players prepared in anticipation of the All-England and, for the rest of the year, enjoyed the charm of invitation tournaments, which were quite popular in those days.

Hartono's first appearance on the Indian courts was sometime in the late sixties, and during one such event, some Indians, too, possessed something to stump a man of his calibre. With his anxiety-prone spin serve that he regularly deployed in nationals, Satish Bhatia took the first game to an otherwise windless visage of Hartono. On Hartono's protest, he had to stop his spin serve, and the Indonesian returned to his regular self and won the next two games. Bhatia's national counterparts may have wished for the same but to little avail!

For his 1969 visit with the Indonesian team for the Thomas Cup first-round match in Jaipur, the BAI put a gymnastics expert to work, a Netaji Subhas National Institute of Sports (NSNIS) coach named Darshan Kumar Tandon, to train and boost their athletes' stamina. A three-month training camp in Rajasthan meant proximity to the spiritually resplendent Mount Abu and the desert. He made the team trek the mountain and track the sands of the desert.

'The concept of physical training didn't exist, and all feats of the human body were tested, exploited and achieved in the badminton court,' in the words of Khanna. The training paid off to the extent that Khanna, whose stamina would test the opponent's failing resolve, beat Muljadi. He was another Indonesian whose robust game made him last two distinct eras of domination in the Thomas Cup, first being 1958 to 1964 and then from 1970 to 1979. Romen Ghosh and Dipu Ghosh, a formidable doubles pair, won too.

But Indonesia managed to dominate the tie at 7–2. Even though the Indians impressed or maybe even startled the Indonesians with their newfound prowess, they still had a long way to go.

Hartono visited India again, in the early 1970s, for the Bombay Gymkhana Invitation tournament where Padukone had to face the Indonesian in the first round. Hartono's majestic smashes and made-to-kill style of play left Padukone in a trance. He was, after all, seeing him for the first time.

Padukone lost to him 15–2 and 15–7 but had already decided to learn as much as possible from the legend. The team went to Jabalpur, where Padukone requested to watch Hartono practice at the team hotel. Early in the morning, he saw Hartono doing skips, ten thousand of those in about one and a half hours and even went on to call it a light workout as he was playing the final in the evening.

Padukone was astonished. He knew he had to surpass his extant game, for which fitness was the most crucial factor. It would make all the difference. Few fitness plans or regimens were in place. But Hartono had stirred the unquenchable thirst within him, and thus, Padukone started idolising him. He began emulating his strokes while practising his 'attacking clear', which turned the defensive stroke into a flatter shot to the baseline.

Hartono could afford an attacking clear, with his speed and mental make-up, to slow down the pace and sync it with his own game. The net dribble had enough momentum in its spin to gift himself the only option of the opponent's lift, which Hartono would end with a resounding smash.

Padukone took over as national coach in 1993 but faced resistance from the BAI when he tried to introduce some new measures. The maestro had plans to revolutionise how the game was conducted and how players were treated.

Padukone didn't want the players to suffer, so he let things be with the BAI.

Padukone, who began by practising badminton in unoccupied wedding halls, today runs a state-of-the-art academy in Bangalore where he coaches aspiring players. Back in 1980, Padukone, on his own, organised a tour for some youngsters from Bangalore to Jakarta to watch the World Championships. This kindness and support earned him immense love and respect in the sporting fraternity. Old-timers recall this event with pride and admiration for Padukone.

8

Syed Modi: A Star's Shining Legacy

CRITICS ACCUSED SYED MODI of being hyped for non-sporting reasons. He hailed from Gorakhpur. Fazil Ahmed, the president of the Badminton Association of India, also did. Modi was talented, ambitious and always up for a challenge, willing to push himself against any opponent. Yet, he was often hurt when many were unwilling to accept him as a player capable of making it to the big stage on the strength of his talent.

Modi backed himself to become the best. He was rustic compared to some of his contemporaries, but he was far more determined. His fellow players remembered his smiling face, but his untiring spirit in confronting the opponents on the court showed Modi as a player to fear. He would take a loss to heart and practise harder to overcome the shortcomings.

His goal was to emulate Padukone, and among his well-known ambitions was to win a contest against the legendary star, which he did in 1980–81 at the National Championship in Vijayawada. Modi ended Padukone's reign and established his own with a rare flourish on the court. Modi was eighteen when he won the national title. He was assassinated eight years later at the gates of the K. D. Singh Babu Stadium, where he had spent his formative years.

Modi was a humble member of the badminton fraternity and had many things in common with Padukone. The ability to translate little openings into victories was Modi's forte; He was a fearless individual who always looked at achieving big. He had a healthy rivalry with Padukone and ultimately achieved his dream of a grand win against his idol.

Padukone and Modi enjoyed a competition that resembled the Connors–McEnroe contests on the tennis court. The legendary matches between Liem Swie King and Han Jian would have the audience on its toes. Tennis fans would well remember the Federer–Nadal era and the Evert–Navratilova summit fights. Of course, Padukone's game was superior to Modi's, but they contributed to popularising the game with their distinct styles.

The final in Vijayawada was a significant moment in Indian badminton. Padukone had been playing in Denmark as a licensed player and had to adjust when he competed at home in the National Championships. As described by S. Thyagarajan of *The Hindu*, Padukone made no excuses. Reporting on the final, Thyagarajan wrote, 'Those who saw Prakash fall from the top position realised that the defending champion was far from his normal self. On the other hand, Modi was simply superb. Prakash, of course, is not given to tantrums or making excuses. He took the defeat in all humility and was the first to praise Modi's triumph.'

According to Shirish Nadkarni, it was clear from the early years that Modi would go far. 'The lad was still a junior when he was included in the Thomas Cup team.' Like Padukone, a young talent made waves in the senior circuit. What stood out was the self-confidence that carried Modi past many hurdles. It suited him that he did not know much about his opponents. He took the court, analysed the opponent and gave his best. There was none like Modi when it came to adapting.

He was born Syed Mehdi Hassan Zaidi, but his name was spelt as Modi at the time of school admission, and the name stuck. But his grave bears the name, a painful reminder to the visitors of a superb career cut short by brutal bullets pumped into his body. The murder shook the badminton world, and his friends found it impossible to accept that a good soul like Modi would meet such an end. Even his rivals nurtured a hidden respect for Modi.

Noted scribe Santosh Suri, who knew Modi personally, wrote in his tribute in *News Nine*, 'I ran into badminton players who were practising with Modi the previous evening, and they gave the details of how Modi and all the boys had a cup of tea at the canteen after the practice session. As Modi drove his scooter outside the gate, they heard gunshots and saw him lying in a pool of blood. How much his fans loved Modi can be gauged from the fact that a huge crowd had gathered at the King George Medical College Hospital in Lucknow, where his body was kept in the mortuary overnight and was released only by noon the following day after a post-mortem examination. Crowds waited patiently for his body to be brought out and carried to the K. D. Singh Babu stadium, ironically the venue of his murder the previous evening. After numerous tributes in Lucknow, his mortal remains were taken to the Gorakhpur graveyard.'

He won the national title eight times, and famously, the crown sat on his head for eight consecutive years, one less than his idol Padukone. It took Modi only a short time to mature as a player because he was a keen learner and never wasted time during camps or travels for competitions. Dinesh Khanna, one of the great players in Indian badminton history, once wrote about Modi in *Sportstar* at the end of a tournament in his early years, 'He is ready to assume the role of an aggressor at the first opportunity, a quality that he sadly lacked earlier.' Modi demonstrated his penchant for attacking at the first opportunity in the second half of his career as his confidence propelled him to great heights.

The year 1982 was the turning point in Modi's career. The gold medal at the Commonwealth Games was the recognition he needed on the big stage. Indian sport was looking up, and this was to mark a decade of achievements. It began with Padukone's All-England title, followed by India hosting the 1982 Asian Games, Kapil Dev's team winning the 1983 World Cup and Sunil Gavaskar leading the side to a triumph at the 1985 World Championship of Cricket. The 1986 Seoul Asian Games saw P. T. Usha claiming four gold medals. It was the best time for young minds planning a career in sports.

For Modi, it was enough reason to justify the faith his predecessors had in him. There was a flourish that marked his movements on the court. He had the grace and the tenacity to match his opponents. He loved to ground the opposition with his untiring stamina. Modi's hard work on the court reflected his sound training.

Modi was the youngest among eight siblings. He had five brothers and two sisters and was the darling of his family. His father, Syed Meer Hassan Zaidi, worked in a sugar mill, and his brothers supported and funded his badminton career. His family believed Modi had the potential to be a global star, and he lived up to their expectations. The Commonwealth gold and the Asian Games bronze in the same year proved Modi's capacity to succeed on the big stage.

'His consistency was his strong point. He had grown as a player in two years, and the victory against Prakash only confirmed his potential. He had the game to unsettle his opponents. His forte was the jump-smash, and I was very impressed with his overall game,' observed Khanna. Most experts believed that Modi had the resilience to emulate Padukone.

Not similar in their play on court, Modi and Padukone had a few common traits. They loved tiring the opponent with their solid defence and a sudden smash. Modi could have been better than Padukone at the net. Padukone was a master at the drop and cross-court placements. Modi would look to stretch the rival, something he had learnt from close observation. Modi also excelled with his backhand, working on this aspect to stun his opponents.

According to Shirish Nadkarni, 'Similarity was between Modi and Goel. Goel took Modi under his wing as his protege. You can see Goel's strokes in Modi's gameplay. Modi's quality of stroke play was far superior to that of Prakash. Prakash had attributes like a powerful mind, excellent temperament and many deceptive strokes. He used to hold his wrist until the last moment and then flick it. His flick toss from the net was exceptionally superb. He could dribble as well as flick behind with the same action. And that is what defeated Liem Swie King in the 1980 All-England final.'

Modi's domination at the national level was complete, like Padukone's. While Modi was alive, the talented Vimal won the title only once. Modi had become the junior national champion when he was just fourteen. His coach, P. K. Bhandari, had trained him well. Padukone had stopped playing in India after the defeat at the hands of Modi, who, however, did not do justice to his talent, winning only three international titles – Austrian Open (1983 and 1984) and USSR Open (1985) – other than the Commonwealth Games gold.

'Being slender and lacking strong shoulders, Modi relied on subtle timing rather than raw power. His game can be compared with tennis star Ramesh Krishnan's style of play, outsmarting the opponents with placements by engaging them in long rallies,' remembered Suri. 'Many compare his game with his fellow Indian Railways badminton star Suresh Goel. Both being at camps together and practising together for hours, Modi picked up the nuances of the game from

Goel. Besides, both were coached by the legendary Dipu Ghosh, thus the similarity in their play.'

Recalling Modi's strong points on the court, Suri noted, 'The advantage of Modi was that he had a powerful backhand, which is generally a weakness with many top players. With a flick of the wrist, he could send the shuttle to the deep corners of the court, to catch the opponents on the wrong foot repeatedly. Because of his stamina, he could hold his own during long rallies and often finished a rally with his patent forehand cross-court half-smash with a jump. That pose appeared in newspapers country-wide time and again during his playing days. Maybe the lack of power did have disadvantages when playing against international players. But there was limited international exposure back then, unlike today's players. If he had been playing in today's times, maybe his achievements would have been far greater.'

According to Sanjay Sharma, Padukone lost to Indian players only once each from 1973 to 1980 – Iqbal Maindargi in 1975 and Modi in 1980. Even though Modi craved good facilities in Uttar Pradesh, his early years of learning the game from Suresh Goel helped him understand the game better. 'Modi was a laidback, cool and calm contender. He had some lovely strokes and an outstanding defence. He would have played much more for India, but for his untimely death.'

For Ameeta, Modi's example and his relationship with Padukone are touching. She claimed never to have seen the kind of respect Modi had for Prakash. 'He always called him Bhai Saab (elder brother) and never took his name. He had the same respect for Suresh Goel, a legend.' Ameeta felt Modi's game was on the lines of Goel. 'Modi learnt the game from Suresh. He respected Ami so much. That is missing today. We had this community living (at camps). Boys and girls going for walks to the gate at Patiala NIS, singing, joking, and teasing. That was the bond. That special feeling of being together.'

Former national junior champion Malvinder Dhillon remembers Modi as a gentleman who would not harm a fly. Modi's calm exterior reflected his inner self. There was nothing that could perturb Modi, not even a close defeat. He would take it in his stride and set out for the next battle. Dhillon said, 'Modi was extremely fit. He would play basketball to improve his flexibility and cycle to attain a high standard of fitness. Modi knew that endurance was an integral part of being a successful player. Modi was a straightforward boy, and I loved him because he made it a point to bring me racquets from his trips abroad. Modi had great respect for the rivals.'

The killing of Modi when he was twenty-five is a dark chapter in Indian sports. He envisioned a career and would have proved a great asset with his deep understanding of badminton. As Dhillon said, 'Modi would have been ideal to groom youngsters because of his work ethic and a solid background of hard work and discipline. We sorely missed his wisdom.'

For Suri, the biggest question that rankled Indian badminton lovers was how Modi's career would have panned out had he not fallen in love with Ameeta Kulkarni and ultimately married her in 1984 when he was twenty-two years old. Modi was at the peak of this prowess then, just about gaining ascendency internationally after having won the 1982 Commonwealth Games gold medal in Brisbane to add to a bronze medal in the 1982 Asian Games in New Delhi. He subsequently won the Austrian Open titles in 1983 and 1984 and the USSR title in 1985.

'He was virtually unbeaten in India from 1980 till his death in 1988, having won the national title eight times in a row, when he defeated Padukone. But his CV is bereft of three major crowns…an Olympic medal, an All-England title and a podium finish in the Thomas Cup,' said Suri.

Modi's friends in his home state have no doubt that Modi could have surpassed Padukone's achievements, won the All-England at least once and have had many more international titles in his kitty. 'There are enough reasons for me to believe that Modi's achievements on his home soil, where he was invincible, are legendary. But a thought always persists in the mind that his career and life would have had many more glorious moments than he ended up with. If he were alive today, he would have undoubtedly guided today's generation like Prakash, Vimal, and Gopi Chand have been doing,' observed Suri.

9

Ameeta Singh: Breaking Barriers with Every Smash

BADMINTON WAS NOT AMEETA'S preferred game. She was a swimmer and represented Maharashtra state. She started swimming at the age of five because her parents believed that children should be physically active. Pursuing a physical activity constructively, regardless of the type of activity, is essential. Therefore, swimming became a part of Ameeta's career. But it could have been smoother for Ameeta. Her grandmother did not appreciate her love for swimming because of the combination of chlorine and sun, gradually forcing her to give it up.

Right next to the Mahatma Gandhi Swimming Pool at Shivaji Park was the Vanita Samaj, which had a badminton court. Ravindra Dongre was the coach at the venue. Ameeta's mother sent her to play badminton, but she returned to the pool. Her brother used to accompany her, and they had a two-hour session. Ameeta's grandmother didn't want her to be in the pool. That's how she started badminton.

Ameeta missed selection to the junior Maharashtra team but went to Calcutta as a sub-junior for her nationals in 1976. She won the sub-junior nationals and became more serious about the game. Ameeta never went to the movies and did not have the temptation of going out with friends. She was fond of reading and would stay focused on sports. She was academically sound since her mother was a professor herself.

Caught between the need to be good at academics and her love for sports, Ameeta worked hard to stay focused. Being a topper, she could practise badminton because the school acknowledged her all-round prowess. Badminton and table tennis were known to bring players together at the long-duration camps. The nature of the competition – teams travelling together – and combinations for the mixed doubles event helped forge many lifelong bonds, and Ameeta was no exception. She found her love in Modi, the brightest star on the Indian badminton horizon after Padukone.

Ameeta and Modi got together in 1980 and married four years later. During that period, they played continuously – Uber Cup, Commonwealth Games, and World Championships. The game saw new champions. The legendary Indonesian Rudy Hartono was giving way to compatriot Liem Swie King. That was the time when badminton was seeing more power games.

International matches were conducted on nova courts, but Ameeta learned the game on wooden floors. It made a significant difference as nova courts offered better grip. You needed at least ten times more power in your legs. The size of the stadium increased your hitting power. It took work to suddenly move from playing in small halls to one with a capacity of 25,000. The dynamics would change. The shuttle's flight would be slower, and you would have to hit harder. These were genuine issues players faced in her era.

One reason players of her era thought Prakash Padukone was phenomenal when he won the All-England was that he had also practised in these circumstances. It was one of the most significant victories in Indian sport.

To gain experience, Ameeta travelled to play the Danish Open and Swedish Open, which were part of the European Circuit. They enjoyed playing test matches against Ireland

and England at that time. It was always a competition of five games – men's singles and doubles, women's singles and doubles, and one mixed doubles. But the exciting part was that the players would travel together, and there was a lot of camaraderie.

It was a great learning experience for the players travelling to Europe. There needed to be more money, and the players would find accommodation at the homes of the local supporters and organisers – two players with one family. It was lovely as the players got to know the local culture. Badminton became a great teacher.

Even though the government funded these trips, the players needed help getting clearances from the government by the time they got their tickets. The last week before departure, when they had to practise, the players would run around for visas and tickets. These uncertainties used to take a toll on the players, who had to encounter a lot of hurdles, but many felt that era was significant. The players were self-disciplined; there was no monetary incentive. And yet, there was so much dedication.

'Ameeta was extremely hard working. I wouldn't say she was limitlessly talented. In terms of talent and hard work one can easily draw a comparison between her and Saina. Saina too had limited talent but had the insight to exploit it to its utmost potential. Ameeta's main problem was a faulty grip, which was not even corrected when she was in the national team. She held the racquet like she was about to chop food with it. Her singles service was faulty because she used to contact the shuttle above the waist level. In fact, during the 1981 All-England, she played against a Korean player. And Ameeta was faulted against her about six times during the match. She became so nonplussed that it cost her the match,' broods Nadkarni.

'There's a proper way to execute the service and hold the racquet. When you take it from the side, bring it down and lift the shuttle to the baseline – you need to make an arc resembling a smile – whereas the trajectory she used to send the shuttle in looked more like a poker face. She often lost out on the international scene because of her faulty service. It must be corrected when the player is young. She was way past the point when it could be improved. Sujata Jain, Ami's first partner, also suffered from a poor grip that was never rectified,' Nadkarni offers an insight at the state of badminton back then.

Modern badminton has transformed the young players into stars. Nearly every badminton player has a manager to promote commercial interests. For Ameeta, this attention garnered by the players was the most pleasant departure from the past. She was delighted for the present generation. During her playing days, she observed that people treated sport as recreation, never a profession.

Ameeta cited an exciting example to make her point: 'I distinctly remember a conversation with Helen Troke (England). She was England's No. 1 at that time. We were watching the All-England finals. I just asked her, 'Helen, what do you do besides playing?' She looked at me in a questioning way and said, 'What do you mean? I play badminton.' I said that I knew but I meant, besides that, what did she do'

'She asked me, 'What do you do besides that?' I replied, 'I study, work and have a job. She asked, 'How do you manage all this?' I said, 'Well, I have to manage all this.' She turned around and told me, 'I don't do anything else. I only play badminton.' And then she told me that, well, if a doctor can't play badminton, a lawyer can't play badminton. Why should I be a doctor or a lawyer?'

The conversation convinced Ameeta that there was a big difference between Indian players and the rest. There was continuous pressure on most of the players of that generation. There was Deepti Thanekar, who got married and went to America to take up a job in a bank. She had to quit the game.

Ameeta followed a rigid schedule – get up by the clock at 4:30 and go to the gym and the beach, finish off at about 8:30 and rush to school. She was allowed to reach school half an hour to forty-five minutes late. That was the concession they had given her in the mornings. Her hard work paid off; she won the sub-junior nationals at fourteen. She never practised with the girls except when she was in the camps and preferred to train with the boys every evening between 5:00 and 8:30 when her dad would pick her up in his car. Ameeta would do her homework during the drive back from Nariman Point to Shivaji Park.

Ameeta loves interacting with today's young badminton players. During the COVID-19 lockdown, she invited some of her contemporaries and current stars for webinar discussions because she lamented the distance between the players. And that is on account of the change in the game. The game had changed, the systems had changed and the academies had come about. The players were only related to one coach, the amount of money invested today was much more and parents expected quick results.

Ameeta's love story with Modi was quite fascinating. They never interacted. For Ameeta Kulkarni, a suave Bombay girl, the rustic Modi was just 'one more player.' She was more with the Maharashtra team, her players and her friends. There was no Modi around.

How did he come into her life then? 'We went to China and played internationals together, but still, we were not in a small team of four or five. It used to be just a pleasantry of, you know, hello and this and that. Whenever sitting together and talking normally like anybody else,' Ameeta confessed, they were 'just colleagues, and nothing else.' The feelings for each other happened in 1980.

At the end of the test series in England, the team was to return to India, and fate played its part. They needed to get bookings on Air India. Ameeta recalled, 'We had to fly only Air India. We got a hopping flight – London–Rome, Rome–Zurich, Zurich–Frankfurt, Frankfurt–Delhi and Delhi–Bombay. Can you believe it? It was like thirty-six hours on an aircraft for an eight-hour flight.'

Fate was bringing Ameeta and Modi together. The aircraft developed a snag during the stopover at Zurich. 'By the way, my seat was next to Syed. Fair enough. I mean, we were all sitting together. We were chatting. The flight was getting delayed. They did not allow us to get off the aircraft. We were sitting in the plane for six hours. Now, after six hours, we were seated, and that's when we started talking because we were stuck. A little about how badminton is in Uttar Pradesh and Maharashtra.'

The story continued as they took off from Zurich and returned to London because of a change of aircraft. Hours were spent boarding again for the flight to India. Ameeta realised that Modi had gone and had gotten the boarding pass with her seat next to him. 'He distinctly got my boarding pass with a seat next to him. We were chatting more than usual on the same route from Zurich to Frankfurt. We were getting to know each other better – about our families and what we do when you know those kinds of questions that normally have never happened between him and me. He left me in Delhi, as I was supposed to go to Bombay. He prayed for my safe flight.'

Modi said something that stuck with Ameeta. 'If you want to play the World Championships, which are pretty close, you better lose weight.'

'I found that very strange. Why did he say something like this to me?' He was a shy person, not outspoken by nature. I didn't say anything. I went back home.' Modi continued to stay in touch through phone calls. 'They were trunk calls those days. You had to book those calls,' she smiled.

Ameeta worked on losing weight before going to the Bangalore camp. At the camp, Modi got friendly with her as they had to walk to the Century Club through Cubbon Park. The two would visit the Tiffany Hotel. 'There was a crooner at Tiffany singing lovely songs. We would go there for a cold coffee, because we realised we wanted to spend time together. We were getting to know each other better.' They developed a deep interest in each other.

The team for the World Championships included Padukone, Modi, Ami, Ameeta and Partho Ganguly. Again, Modi and Ameeta looked to spend time together. When she returned from Jakarta, Ameeta told her mother she was 'interested' in Modi. Her mother did not take Ameeta seriously, as she was just eighteen.

If Ameeta's mother thought it was a settled matter, she was wrong. Ameeta persistently conveyed to her mother that she was fond of him. The media reported that Ameeta and Modi were dating. Now was the time for her parents to step in. They spoke to Modi's brother. They decided to get engaged.

Religion was never an issue for them. Ameeta said, 'It was hard to say he was a Muslim. He lived in Gorakhpur, where Sikhs surrounded him. I lived in a lazy town with wonderful people for a long time. If I could not do the puja, he would do the puja. Religion was never a subject that came up between the two of us. Never. He gave me a Taveez (good luck charm). Syed kept it in his pocket and would constantly touch it during matches. I also used to keep it in my pocket. That was a big bonding thing for us. Syed was not a very religious person, and I am secular.'

Ameeta was a courageous young woman who was aware of the challenges she would face. Her decision was not something that people would readily accept, especially given her conservative Brahmin background. However, her parents were open-minded, and there was no opposition from either side. Modi's family was also incredibly welcoming.

Modi and Ameeta spent a great time together and became involved in each other's game. In fact, she was more engaged in his game, pushing him a lot. On the court, his footwork was phenomenal. He was a certainty in every team because he was unbeaten after beating Padukone. The only match he lost before being assassinated was against Vimal Kumar. 'And that was the match he told me he would lose,' Ameeta remembered. It was some selection tournament in Bareilly, and Ameeta had not accompanied him because she was expecting their first baby. When he was leaving, Modi expressed his worry to her, 'I hope I don't end up losing.' And he did. After that defeat, he beat Vimal.

Ameeta and Modi were married in 1984 in Lucknow, two years after he won the Commonwealth Games gold in Australia. The final happened on October 4, which was Ameeta's birthday. When Modi insisted on giving her a gift, she asked for the gold medal. He had become weak from a fever, and Ameeta was granted special permission to visit him at the boys' hostel.

Every day, he lost weight and collapsed on the court during practice. He made a remarkable recovery to win the gold after a final that lasted an hour and forty-six minutes. 'I felt happy when everyone congratulated me for getting him to the courts.'

Two miscarriages upset Ameeta and Modi. She was away from badminton. 'I had lost nine months in two pregnancies. I had gained weight; I was out of shape. The press had written me off. I wanted to play, but I wanted a baby. It was a very turbulent time for me mentally. And for him also because he was seeing me suffer. Syed convinced me to get back to the game. I started playing again. And I became India's No. 1 again. I came back with one condition: the moment the nationals were over, I will find family again.'

Ameeta had made up her mind to have a baby, 'I consciously put my racquets up. It was not unplanned or an error. I said, give me one year, and I'll be back. And then I had Aakanksha. Immediately after that, the shootout happened. I lost him, and I was in no frame to think of badminton then. The first couple of years were draining,' she recalled.

Modi's life was cut short on 28 July 1988, when he was shot dead in Lucknow at the K. D. Singh Babu Stadium. It sent the sporting fraternity into a state of shock. Things got worse for Ameeta when she was charged with murder along with politician Sanjay Singh by the police.

'After he was shot, I started feeling that the next person would be me. It was a very insecure period. Pain, anger, loss, every negative word that you can use was part of me at that time, except that I was not negative. I was very, very quiet. My personality was not the person I was. I had just become reticent. I was not meeting anybody. I was not talking to anybody, just to myself.'

It was a nightmare for Ameeta. 'By then, I didn't know I was fighting a government. I understood politics and the CBI, so I knew what the CBI was doing. Everything was crystal clear in front of my eyes. What had happened, and why was it done? Let me tell you that the case never started.'

'Regarding the legal side, the CBI was on the case. The CBI filed the charge sheet, and the Lower Court dismissed it. The high court and the Supreme Court rejected the charge sheet. Then, they appealed for a special review before the Chief Justice. The Chief Justice dismissed it too. It was eight years of going through this.'

Ameeta alleged that the government turned it into a political issue. 'They wanted to frame him (Sanjay Singh). Today, no one knows who killed him. Of course, we know who killed him. But officially, it never came out because they did not want it to come out. Eight years went by in that battle. I could not have gotten back to the game. I was not in a frame to return. We got married eight years later (1995).

After marriage, I went to Amethi and started working there. And then I entered politics myself.'

Ameeta's initiation into politics was natural since she did a lot of social work, such as conducting medical camps and managing schools. In 2000, she contested her first election and became chairman of the zilla panchayat. She fought the election to the Assembly and won; she was made a minister for education. She calls herself a full-time politician.

How much does she remember the time spent with Modi? 'They are the most memorable moments. It was so much fun. They called us lovebirds in Lucknow. We would always try to wear the same attire: the same tracksuits, T-shirts, shoes, and caps. People would stop us on the roads. We had a car, but we used to ride a bike. People would stop us and ask for autographs.'

Ameeta recalled the fond moments spent with Modi. 'I used to refer to him as Jaanu (my beloved) instead of his official name, Modi. However, I preferred to address him as Syed. Although he enjoyed playing cards, I never liked it as I found it distracting.' He loved ghazals and carried a lot of music with him. He always had that dual Walkman with earphones. 'I still have that Walkman. All those memories of how I would be cooking, and he would be sitting on the kitchen slab, distracting me more than anything else. I remember furnishing that house with him. It was such fun. We earned our money to provide the place. We decided to not take any support from my parents. So that furnishing part was also a great time. Then we bought our first car – a Maruti 800. I still have it.'

Modi is still an essential part of Ameeta's life. 'Even today, I've got every possession that we both shared. If you go to my daughter's room, you will see all he brought from the Commonwealth Games. My microwave oven, which is running in this kitchen, is what we bought. We bought the washing machine in my Lucknow house, which is still running – every possession I have treasured. And Sanjay treasures them too. There's never any fear of talking about Syed. I have my coffee maker from that house. Even the crystals I picked up from Moscow are still with me. All the things that we had are still a part of my life. But that period was challenging. Many athletes were scared of being questioned if they met me. But I did not hold anything against anybody.'

There was a brief temptation for Ameeta to return to the badminton court. She played once in 2008, when her daughter was about four years old. 'I had to prepare her to grow up and face this whole thing. It was also essential to my mind that I had to prepare her to face what I had gone through. I was not ready to compromise her at any stage, because the world was very harsh. I spent a lot of time with her. I wanted her to understand things as age permitted.'

Every few months her daughter would ask something new. Then, Aakanksha saw the case papers after doing her masters in criminal litigation. And the day she came back from England after her masters was the first time she asked her parents, 'Can I take a look at that damn case?'

As Ameeta recalled, 'She said, I wish I had been a lawyer, then I would have represented you. Aakanksha is now a successful criminal lawyer thanks to her time with Mr (Ram) Jethmalani. As a five-year-old, she would climb into his chair and study the room. She had a fascination for books. She thought being a lawyer meant you got books. She was in eighth grade when she decided to become a lawyer. She was a voracious reader. She needed me growing up, and there was no way I would go back and play badminton.'

Ameeta advocates the importance of sports in her interactions with people. 'I would recommend sports to every child.' She has ten institutions (18,000 students) in Amethi, which she set up after marriage. 'I make it a point that they play. Whether they win or lose, they must participate because the whole idea is to be able to accept defeat. A winner is a winner, but the person who can accept defeat is a complete human being. You can never be a winner everywhere. There are ups and downs in everybody's life. The moment you can accept defeat, you learn to win the next time you compete.'

There is much to suggest that she was once a graceful badminton star. She presents a far more engaging countenance as a politician, even as badminton seems ingrained in her character. She spends time commuting between Delhi and her constituency in Uttar Pradesh, but badminton is integral to her life. She can't miss her daily yoga session. 'I gave up on a lot of food to keep my fitness. I have not had rice in thirty years.'

Remembering that critical phase (Modi's murder) in her life, Ameeta said, 'Obviously, when this episode happened, everyone was in a state of shock, but I cannot tell you how affectionate his family has been. They have stayed in touch with me, which half the world doesn't know.'

Ameeta has returned to badminton as an administrator, organising tournaments in Delhi and ensuring players have access to the best possible facilities as they pursue their dreams.

10

Ami Ghia: Magic on the Court

THE YEAR WAS 1968. She would return from school, keep her bag in its usual place, change into her routine clothes and stride out, but only after grabbing her racquet and reaching the compound of her house. Soon, her friends would join her. She had many, or enough, to complete a court of badminton. Those friends would play a significant role in the history of women's badminton. This she didn't know at that time, nor did she care. She was playing to have a good time on the court. She loved holding the racquet, feeling its grip to accost the shuttle where she intended to.

For Ami Ghia, it started as a hobby but soon became a part of her being. It is hard to know if it was caught during the small adventures of childhood – like grasping a butterfly's wings with the fringe of a child's fingers – or if it was just there all along, dormant and silent. It will be hard to find the answer, but she is thankful for the journey.

She was eleven then, and a neighbour who used to watch her game during those afternoon escapades identified her talent. He suggested to her father that he make her join a local club in the suburbs of Bombay called Khar Gymkhana. Her father didn't see any reason to not to, and thus, she started playing badminton there. There were two categories: those below eighteen and those above. Joining the first was convenient and mandatory, as her school wound up around half past three. It was only a matter of time, though not much, before she would be requesting the adults off the courts. But grabbing a shuttle for practice was a challenge! A shuttle was given to them every half an hour. Thankfully, her home was close to the gymkhana, which used to help her clinch the bird.

Inspiration from someone was less of a reason for Ami to stay with badminton, if not completely invalid. With TV broadcasting still in its infancy, it was challenging to idolise successful people. She may have gradually heard of a few names in badminton making rounds when she plunged into the competitive circuit. Still, it was not enough to stir her imagination. The game came to her naturally, like a gush of a pleasant breeze.

Ami didn't set goals when envisaging herself five or ten years later. There was no pressure from her parents either, so she breezed through each day as it arrived. She participated in and won local tournaments and was soon playing for Bombay, and then Maharashtra was to follow. She credits a gentleman appointed to coach for one summer camp at Khar gym. 'The badminton aspect of my game improved through his mentoring,' she believes.

She had two sisters, both of whom were studying medicine. When Ami tried to remember how it all fell into place, it often felt blurry to the listener, as if it were more a matter of destiny than intent. She chose to ride the wings of her talent with her hard work and commitment to the sport. Since television and the influence of the media were meek, eyes still needed to be glued to screens. It also meant limited awareness of potential career opportunities. However, her parents had the essential ingredient, and that was support. Her sisters were into dance and music, but their parents never raised eyebrows about Ami wanting to follow a different path. The path led to an impressive haul of seven singles titles at the nationals.

Ami was to bring back the thrill of women's badminton, which was felt almost a decade ago. Meena was a prolific champion, and there was no opponent during her prime to stop her. This did not mean women's badminton was lagging when Damayanti started ruling the national courts for three consecutive years. But with Ami's entry, the country experienced a déjà vu.

There will be comparisons and distinctions analysed against her predecessors while always remembering that Ami was a born star. She consecutively participated in the nationals on nineteen occasions, out of which fifteen times she appeared in the singles finals. Her national debut was when she was only fourteen. This record speaks of the permanency of Ami's image for about two decades in the national charts and people's hearts. Being a consecutive winner like Meena is a lore. Still, Ami displayed grit in her comebacks and refused to back down.

'Ami was naturally talented and very hard working. She played all three events, which presently no one does. This meant she had the potential to win fifty-seven titles. She was in thirty-six finals and she won twenty-three titles. That is a record that no one will ever come close to, let alone beat it,' says Nadkarni in his most emphatic voice. Lack of brute physical strength resulted in disappointment in the international circuit. She used to run into stronger players while representing India and they would wear her out. 'Her best chance used to be winning in straight games otherwise if the match went into the third game, she would find it too hard to finish with a victory.' Nadkarni provides a glimpse into what could have been.

Her early participation in tournaments dates back to when she played at Khar Gymkhana. The club and Bandra Gymkhana, which finds itself in the eponymous suburb of Bandra, used to hold their tournaments. People who witnessed her game would recall her on the court as steady and balanced with her feet instead of baffling her rivals with swift movements. However, she had other abilities to achieve the same. But her entry into the nationals scene was a dazzling sprint.

In 1970, she played her first nationals in Hyderabad. She toppled her opposition to win the junior doubles with her close friend Sujata Jain. They knew each other from their practice sessions at Khar Gymkhana. Ami used her practice time well when playing against Sujata. She used her strategies during those encounters, improved her command over them and raised her bar for the game and, consequently, her confidence during the tournaments. Sujata had power and speed in her inventory, which proved advantageous for Ami to battle against while enriching her game.

Junior and senior nationals were still organised simultaneously and at the same venue. Both the girls proved daunting enough for the selectors to facilitate an early entry into the women's category. At the 1971 nationals, Ami won both the junior singles and doubles. In the singles, she had met with Kanwal, who would become one of the most formidable contenders. She took the doubles title with Sujata, and to their delight, they were also given their first entry into the women's doubles event. But as much as it was an achievement, it did come with some disappointment for some, as these two girls fell short in the seniors while trying to pace themselves to the speed and prowess of their older counterparts.

Ami made a stunning impression in the 1972 nationals held in Guwahati. In the singles, she beat Shobha, the defending champion, to win the semifinals. The final was against Rafia Latif. Despite a challenging game, Ami refused to give up. Ami was on the verge of winning the match point when Rafia outsmarted her with her swift on-court moves. Ami was only sixteen at the time.

Without making any noise, she ensured all the reigning women's champions felt struck by her presence and that she was there to stay. A new name in the books was welcome. In the juniors, she took on Sujata in the final but lost. As if nothing had happened, they combined to take their camaraderie to the girls' doubles finals and were successful. The pair even made it to the women's doubles finals against the formidable wall of Shobha and Maureen Mathias. They finished second.

Then came her peak. She was an unstoppable force that one could sense on the court but never mistakenly assume to be a brute. She had no discernible weaknesses. She knew exactly how to work her opponent's strength. The 1973 Gorakhpur nationals was the first in her four-year streak, not that she would stop at the record. She took the singles category by storm.

Badminton was her love, and playing singles was her strength, but making oneself participate in doubles would ensure a higher medal tally – exposure to varied styles of play and players that the game had to offer – and an opportunity to make friendships that would last a lifetime. She claimed the women's doubles title thrice in 1974, 1975 and 1976, with Maureen being her affiliate in all three years. Things were going too well to be true.

Her singles streak was cut short rather cruelly in the 1977 nationals. Otherwise, Ami could achieve the straight line of victories projected by Meena first, Madhumita in the mid-1980s and Aparna later. Kanwal entered the frame and dictated the singles crown for two years straight, and both times put Ami's tested strategies to rest. Ami shook hands with an imposing opponent she hadn't witnessed before and had to make do with the status quo for the time being. Ami quickly realised she might as well pair up with Kanwal in the doubles and use her prowess to claim a win. The pair succeeded in taking the women's doubles title in 1978, the year Ami lost to Kanwal in the singles final. The two came together to win bronze in the doubles at the Commonwealth Games (1978) and the team event at the Asian Games (1982).

Her game mystified people back then and continues to do so when her compatriots try to recall her confidence on the court. Her younger peers carried the same appreciation to the next generation. She was known to put just the right amount of effort into her strokes that would lead the shuttle exactly to its intended spot. She had grace in her movement, though small-framed, and her presence never caused even a trace of anxiety in her fans due to her lack of power. Her wrist commanded the racquet like a wand when the right spell would come immediately, enough to leave her opponent stupefied. She had mastered her footwork to let the strokes control the shuttle, not vice versa.

An amusing fact about her, which moved from ear to ear in the badminton circuit, was her befuddling longing to face aggressive and attacking players. If given a choice, she would always choose the form, as mentioned earlier, of opposition as she had the perfect ploy to diffuse the rage from the other end, and use their force to claim as her own. If the shuttle came at her with vigour, she would use sharp angular placements that would defy all efforts put in by her rival. To further stump them, she aimed the shuttle at their bodies with a half smash, which would paralyze most of the players. And if the attack didn't work against her, she would employ defence with a high clear shot to press the shuttle to the baseline with a bow-like trajectory. But to finally end her sorcery, she would immobilise the rival with a perfectly placed drop, hitherto unforeseen. That was the magic of Ami.

According to Sanjay Sharma, 'Ami was the most graceful player on the court with a fantastic selection of shots. She was precise with exceptional deception. I have hardly seen a player with the same level of deception. Ami was a great player to watch. She would put you on your wrong foot each time with her controlled strokes. She was not a hard hitter but a precise hitter.'

Ami's acknowledgement of Kanwal goes back to their junior nationals days, and she refuses to credit their doubles companionship as the beginning of their friendship. Being gifted badminton players, Ami and Kanwal enjoyed opportunities to travel and represent their states. They were introduced to each other at different stages – formally as peers, later through rivalry and finally as a chapter in each other's stories.

As Ami fondly recalls what constituted her training in her nascent days, she finds herself jogging by the bleached waves of Juhu beach in Bombay. At the same time, the cool draughts of the breeze remind their companions of how beautiful life is. Her parents take a walk while she sprints down the shore carefree.

At Khar gym, she had glanced at someone skipping, and they suggested she could benefit from investing time in the activity. And with that, she also caught the skipping bug, although it was advantageous when not performed in copious amounts. Soon, she and her mates were introduced to weight training.

In the camps for the nationals, they came across exercises for the tracks and specific drills for the court. When she established her position in the game and started working for the railways in 1973, there was a volleyball coach who understood how aspects of physical training were transferable to badminton or any other sport. He used to take the team to the beach to impart his training, and the significance of fitness was further affirmed for Ami. 'It was here that I learnt how much training was required by my body to firstly maintain the fitness level and then to improve upon what was already achieved by my mind,' said Ami.

Leroy said he valued Ami's contribution more than Madhumita's. 'Ami used to play for Maharashtra State. The interstate championship used to be held the week before the individual nationals. She was always the key player. She had to play singles and doubles to try to win the titles for Maharashtra. She used to be tired when the individual nationals culminated, but Madhumita did not play in the interstate championship. Most of the time, Madhumita sat it out. She played the individuals. And there was so much pressure on Ami. She was a strong player, no doubt at all. But that is where Ami was at a disadvantage because she was a team player,' Leroy remembered.

It would be only in the late 1970s when Padukone, with his eagle eye, used a splendid opportunity to visit Indonesia and see the rock-hard Hartono upfront in his training sessions. He worked at the Union Bank. The deputy general manager was a keen admirer of Padukone and wanted to help further his career. On Padukone's request, Union Bank relayed the plea to the BAI, which then reached out to the Indonesian authorities. Modi, the next big name in the men's squad of India, was also granted the chance to accompany Padukone and witness first-hand what goes inside the factory where legends like Hartono and Liem Swie King were cast with steely resolve.

They watched the Indonesians, who had a separate physical trainer, with Hartono being the epitome of physicality. Whatever he did was always double what the two could manage. Be it 400-metre runs, skipping or bench presses, Hartono was way ahead. The boys did improve considerably in stamina and speed through their strenuous training in Indonesia. They tasted the work that went into becoming world champions.

Amid all the passion and commitment, balancing work, family life, and the unavoidable drudgery that routine generally swamps one with, friendship, for Ami, proved a powerful tool to keep up the motivation for the game. Like always, having a friend was important even then. The times were more straightforward, with innocence splayed out in carefree jokes, unadulterated care for each other, an understanding of the limited resources, and the spirit of competition.

Ami, for all generation of players, remains a picture of poise and a spirit that binds opponents on and off the court. It is generally felt that Ami could have contributed immensely by nurturing young players. But family commitments kept her busy off the court even though she followed the game on television to keep herself in tune with modern badminton. When the Indians are in action, you can be sure Ami would be following them from the comforts of her home in Mumbai.

11

Kanwal Thakar Singh: Shaping the Court with Strength

A STRIKING YET SOLITARY, modest yet bold and happy-go-lucky girl made waves in the unadorned badminton world. Born in Delhi, Kanwal Thakar Singh spent a memorable portion of her childhood in the palatial Red Fort, built in 1639 by the Mughal emperor, Shah Jahan. It was his palace for the capital, Shahjahanabad. And Shahjahanabad is Old Delhi or 'Purani Dilli', as they call it now, the house of Mughal mansions and delicacies. This was a walled city, like the palace at its centre. Red Fort was fortified with red sandstone, and its architectural design inspired many constructions that came later in the north of India, like in Kashmir, Punjab and Rajasthan.

Her father, Colonel Thakar Singh, an army officer, was stationed in Delhi for some time. Senior-ranked officers enjoyed the beauty of housing quarters inside the Red Fort. Ample space was everywhere; royal beds proudly rested in rooms, antique furniture would adorn long drawing rooms to host influential guests, and everything one could picture when Mughal palaces came to mind. Kanwal saw it all and lived it all. It remains a fond memory for her.

Her mother, Mrs Diljit Thakar Singh, had a tall personality and exuded elegance. While in school, Diljit was looked up to and admired by other girls her age. She was engrossed in sports during her growing years. With squash and tennis lessons filling her routine when she was young, one would not be too surprised to know she excelled academically and was the head girl in school. She was awarded the title of best athlete in college and would go on to represent her state after marriage. Kanwal's father used to play hockey when he was in the army. Her memory of seeing her parents attending tennis and squash classes together is etched in her mind.

After Delhi, they were stationed in Meerut, Uttar Pradesh. There was a Wheeler's club where one could swing a racquet, dip oneself in a pool, entertain friends and family over drinks and food, or meet other army men. Mainly, one would find people belonging to the defence forces, rarely from different walks of life. It was maintained in the cantonment area. It is generally found draped in garlands during weddings or decked up with lights during private parties. But back then, having access to the club symbolised a certain status in society. An ordinary man would not be allowed in, and thus, 1960s kids who were lucky to find themselves in the courtyards of such clubs have fond memories.

Kanwal would frequent the club every afternoon and evening, where she and her sister learnt swimming. Her father ensured they used the pool well and gave them swimming lessons. Good fitness was achieved by benefiting from what each sport had to offer. Putting to use and working out different sets of muscles in various environments and against varying resistances made Kanwal the epitome of physique and stamina back then. It was a treat for the audience to come and watch her play.

Mrs Thakar Singh was a badminton enthusiast who enjoyed a daily session. This point in Kanwal's life would be written as a milestone. The lioness had tasted blood, and many will be observing her trail. Her mother played badminton in the evening, and Kanwal didn't miss the opportunity to watch. She was only four and a half at that time. Kanwal used to wait patiently for the elders to clear the courts, and once they were tired, she would enter with the 'marker' and toss around the shuttle with him for as long as she could. She wasn't whiling away running, screaming or pulling hair like a regular child. Always looking forward to the racquet and the court, Kanwal found the perfect grip the first time she held the racquet. And it was natural that she was flipping her wrist to flex her picks and strokes in no time. Her sister would accompany them, but not as regularly as Kanwal did. She had other plans in mind.

Given her father's nature of work, another relocation had to happen sooner or later, and Meerut would someday be the cause of nostalgia. They shifted to Ambala from Meerut and embraced it as their next home. Ambala is not a metropolis, but it does enjoy the stature of a small city in Haryana. Badminton tailed Kanwal there as well, or vice versa could be true. Kanwal stalked it till she had found it, to her delight. Whichever may be the case, destiny made sure they both met each another. Here, Kanwal had more time with the racquet, and on the court, she was spending two to three hours at a stretch with no thought in mind other than making the shuttle dance to her melody.

She liked skating too and had huge open spaces or verandahs at her disposal. As if this was not enough, she participated in sprints and other races in her new school. With vivid memories of life at that age, she remembers being above average in academics, if not exceptional. She had even received a double promotion during one of their timely migrations. But she doesn't consider herself as intelligent as her sister. Her hard work helped Kanwal bridge any gap she might have felt. 'I was able to pour my heart into everything I laid my hands and set my eyes on,' said Kanwal with a smile that reflects pride.

Her mother wasn't just playing evening badminton. She wanted more out of it. She used to participate in the Ambala district tournament and was a verified threat. Her triple crown victories, which meant usurping each title (singles, doubles and mixed doubles), told a lot about her game and herself. She used to match with an army officer and his wife for mixed and women's doubles, so she was left alone when he got a call for his next posting. Being the reigning queen, she was comfortably adjusted to getting ordained with the triple crown. She didn't want to bind herself to playing only singles.

During a visit to the courts, administrators from the district association pleaded too many times with her to bless the tournament with her participation. 'I was nine and a half and still sucking on my thumb, sitting in a chair when my mother offered me as a replacement for her,' recalls Kanwal. Her mother knew she had it in her, and the administrators, although reluctant, allowed her to play. Kanwal slaughtered all her opponents.

Soon, it was time for another posting for her father, and now they were off to Jabalpur, a city in Madhya Pradesh. Obeying the pattern, it is easy to guess her mother found a club there by the name of Narmada quite quickly. The girls had to follow their mother. Afternoons and evenings were usual – swimming preceded badminton. Kanwal again was not limiting herself only to the sports that she was exposed to by her parents; by now, she had moved up to participating in hurdles.

Having grown taller and having developed more strength in her thighs, she was preparing herself to slog more. One fine day, Chadha ran into them during a practice session as he, too, was a club member and suggested they should participate in the Madhya Pradesh state tournament. Nothing could make them happier, and they readily registered themselves in the tournament.

Kanwal made her mark in junior singles. With her sister, she claimed the junior doubles title. Mrs Thakar Singh kept her distance from playing singles for her reasons. She couldn't find a better partner than her daughter for the doubles category. And with that, they also took home the senior women's doubles title. From here on, at twelve, Kanwal represented Madhya Pradesh at the junior level for roughly a year and played in an inter-state tournament in Bombay.

Soon, she went for the Madras nationals, where her father kept her company. Richard Purser, a New Zealand badminton player, had participated in the nationals that year. It was an open tournament, so a non-Indian entry was eligible. But for Kanwal, it was an early disappointment as she faced defeat at the hands of Jesse Phillips in the first round. But as a famous saying goes, 'opportunities are like sunrises'; there was already a lot destined for her future.

Her father retired when in Jabalpur, and finally, they decided to settle in Chandigarh. Badminton was the last thing that could be left behind. He had met Sardar Narottan Singh in Madras during the nationals, with whom he hit it off almost instantly. It was something that was a given as they were both Punjabis! Knowing their plan to settle in Chandigarh, Mr Singh suggested to her father that he be on the lookout for Punjab's badminton tournament, which was supposed to begin its registration process soon.

An interesting observation about her early career is that she represented the states first instead of playing in school or college tournaments. In Jabalpur, she was studying at St Joseph's Convent School. The school administration was apprised of their recent triumph after reading about them in the dailies and called Mrs Thakar Singh to request and make her daughters participate in games planned by it. The trio already had a little fame glued to their names.

Initially, coming to Chandigarh only elicited feelings of what they were missing from before.

For the first time, they were experiencing civilian life. 'Cantonment life with clubs, Air Force and army officers is beautiful. There is no better way to put it. Civil life differs sadly,' Kanwal says. Her mother constantly coaxed her father to consider settling in Ambala, only a thirty to thirty-five minute trip from Chandigarh. Retired officers and even their children who followed in their fathers' footsteps feel that being an armed forces officer was much better back then. The facilities in her time were commonplace for people with an army background.

Soon, her mother read in a newspaper that a hall with badminton facilities was opening in Sector 7. She packed everyone in the car, and they were off to witness the hall provisions with high expectations of the charm the English clubs had previously offered them. On reaching the courts, they discovered it was not stately, but they realised it was okay, too. But there was something that struck a jarring chord with Kanwal. 'Men did not stand up upon seeing my mother, and not just my mother per se but any lady,' said an exasperated Kanwal, with a scowl on her face.

It was customary or a gentlemanly etiquette in the armed forces to stand and greet whenever a woman entered the room. It didn't matter how often the door swung open to let a woman in or what crucial point they made in an amusing conversation. The men just did it with grace. A senior police officer crossed his indifferent legs when he saw Mrs Thakar Singh and looked away. Kanwal didn't like it and pulled a sneering face at him. But this was the civilian life they had only heard and dreaded being a part of. This would happen often, but Kanwal never stopped pointing it out to those men. Sometimes, to little avail. She was never intimidated by the thought of putting her foot down.

Her mother's influence on her life is unmissable. Giving importance to sports, choosing a wardrobe that put forth the poise of the woman wearing it, and being mad about badminton, there must have been an idol to imbibe all of these from. Her mother used to dress herself in resplendent saris and sometimes sleeveless blouses. It tells us about the independence she had and how much of it was offered by the era.

A portrait was made of hers for which she decided to dress rather modestly. 'Ma, but this is not who you are,' Kanwal protested. But her mother only liked that picture of herself. She wanted it to be mounted on the wall to remind anyone who came to their home of her beauty and the terms by which she lived, told through the earnest words of her daughter. She laid a firm groundwork on which Kanwal built her name and style. What she chose was always up to her. She was introduced to badminton by her mother, but she decided to stay with it. She showed her love for the game by training for hours on end.

Even at home, she couldn't rest peacefully. Their house attendants used to get a much-needed break when Kanwal put them to work and asked them to be her working partners. But if chores didn't allow them, it didn't mean Kanwal had to suspend her determination. She would stringently hit the shuttle at the wall until it breathed its last and wore down to a bald cork. She could do it all alone. The hall was near their home, and Kanwal made herself a regular there. Her sister, on the other hand, was a rare face and showed up typically right before the matches. Kanwal participated in the Punjab state tournament at fourteen and won all the titles one could bag.

Kanwal was mystified by Rudy Hartono, the Indonesian great. She had the opportunity to observe him on court and gather what could be from his off-court dalliances and the on-court raids. The entire Indian team used to sit and watch him train while in Jabalpur, and here, he didn't offer himself any discount and would go on to finish 30,000 skips. 'He was so fit…and to top that, he was incredibly humble and sweet in nature,' exclaims an effusive Kanwal.

Inspired by his discipline and physique, Kanwal would wake up before any rooster could and hit the track to jog at 4:30 a.m., with no respite even in the winters. Winter in the north of India can sting, especially if you are in the neighbourhood of the Himalayan range, which exhibits its magnificent mountains of high gradient in twelve states of India and extends from the state of West Bengal and Arunachal Pradesh in the east, spans Uttarakhand and Himachal Pradesh and finally culminates in Jammu and Kashmir in the north. Other states share only minor parts of their land with the range.

Chandigarh, neighbouring Himachal Pradesh, gets chilly in wintertime. When it was dark outside, Kanwal used to ignite the fuel inside of her to explore the world with a compelling desire to increase her fitness. A lap of an athletics track is 400 metres, so four laps meant 1 mile (1.6 km). Kanwal would finish 25–30 laps steadily, totalling 12 kilometres. She would religiously follow the same routine each morning without fail, starting with sprints, strides and a few other exercises such as high knees, where one has to walk by lifting their knee to their chest and touch it with their palm, to be followed by the other knee. From here, her next destination would be the courts.

On alternate days, she had to practise what is quite common in the adolescent days of badminton: shadow drills. In this, one emulates the play and shots they would typically use in a match but without a shuttle. The player practises all kinds of strokes, like picks, drops, tosses, and even shots, using the correct number of steps combined with the proper alignment and positioning of the feet. A coach or a peer just points where the imaginary shuttle flew one after the other. A family friend of her parents, a court manager, used to take the initiative for Kanwal and always encouraged her to play and train more and more. She had won the hearts of almost everyone at the courts. They adored her training regimen.

Then she had to head to college and, upon returning, rile her mother up because of her afternoon reading sessions. 'You have been awake since 4 a.m.; your body needs some sleep...go sleep!' would be her mother's words in rebuttal. From here, she would go for her evening games. But before playing her singles, she had more exercise in mind – 10,000 skips every day! She would make the generous security guard count the jumps. She would count, too, but the guard was just to ascertain the number. He even started waiting for her to begin her routine so he could escape into the picturesque world of counting jumps!

Much later in her sporting career, she realised that a sport like badminton, which required stamina to survive the load of unrelenting rallies, mainly needed a solid core to be agile and reach the shuttle before it swept the floor. The need for skipping and intensive running was less than Kanwal had thought. It had put undue stress on her knees, which an athlete wakes up to only in the later years. Dinesh Khanna said, 'I do not ask my students to focus more on long-distance running, which is nonsensical. Instead, one must become swift and agile with shuttle running and strength training.'

Sanjay Sharma said, 'Since she was not strong on feet, Kanwal relied greatly on smashes. She would have achieved much if she had hit with pinpoint accuracy.'

A formidable competitor, Kanwal loved her rivalry with the rest. 'I don't think I lost to Madhumita more than once. I remember losing two finals to Ami. Madhumita was very erratic, but Ami was calm. It was tough to play Ami. She was very controlled, and she would not make errors quickly. Ami had a fascinating deception. The stance would show one side, and she would toss the shuttle the other way. At the net, she had the art of twisting the shuttle. That was her pet stroke. Even her toss was so deceptive. Negative points took work to get from Ami,' stated Kanwal. Ami's service was to perfection. Ami was a no-nonsense person. She was so dedicated and focused. Kanwal was the opposite, having fun.

'We got along brilliantly. Madhumita was quick and an outstanding doubles player. She managed singles, doubles and mixed doubles very well. There was Radhika (Bose), tall but she would not stretch. I would look beyond capacity, but Radhika played easy. She is a doctor now in the US. Ami, Madhumita and I had our tensions too,' recalls Kanwal. The players always behaved well with each other. With limited badminton events in the country and certain talented players earmarked for them, including the national camps, they faced each other on the court. They happily shared a room during camps and tours. This exposed them to each other's quirks and made them understand each other beyond the dividing lines of the court.

Kanwal is considered an enigma in Indian badminton. Two national titles in singles and two in doubles do not justify her hard work and dedication. Her international feats came in the form of a bronze medal in women's doubles at the 1978 Commonwealth Games with Ami as her partner. They repeated the medal four years later at the Asian Games in Delhi in the team event. She also won the mixed doubles bronze in Leroy's company. According to some experts, she was an underachiever, considering her talent. On the court, she was the epitome of endurance. Combined with her skills and temperament, Kanwal should have had a more significant run, but she chose to end her career and settle down to married life in the United States. Kanwal has stayed in touch with her dear friend Ami, and their endearing friendship only reflects the healthy state of the competition during their times.

12

Hufrish Nariman: The Charming Dissenter

There is an air of assertiveness about Hufrish Nariman. Her kind countenance is infectious, and her smile and laughter are endearing qualities that mark her personality. It's hard to imagine she was once a firebrand player. 'I have mellowed quite a bit,' she said, reflecting on a career full of ups and downs. One of the many unsung contributors to the game, Hufrish has maintained her connection with badminton by devoting time to training young aspirants at the Cricket Club of India (CCI).

Her voice is soft, and one has to strain to catch what she says. Like most girls from her era, Hufrish indulged in more than one sport. 'I used to play cricket when they started the game with Diana (Edulji) and her sister (Behroze) at the CCI. I used to play hockey, too. Then I took up badminton,' she recalled.

For the first five years, Hufrish lived in Dadar, a predominantly Marathi-speaking area in Mumbai, before moving to the Parsee Colony in Byculla. 'They used to have a badminton court there. We would play there and at school (J. B. Vachha) in Dadar. It was a makeshift court where I started playing regularly. In my time, we didn't have under-13 or under-15. It was straight under-18. I probably started when I was eight years old.'

Most Parsi colonies have good facilities for children to play. Some of them have good club houses and decent badminton courts. Her parents put Hufrish in coaching at the Elphinstone Club in Victoria Terminus. 'The place had a good marker (Laxman Salvi) who used to play with the foreigners when they would visit the club for matches. I learnt all the strokes from him. I also went to Homi Talyarkhan. And then I met Mr Pramanik. He was an NIS coach. He had come for one of our school nationals and was available in Bombay at IIT, Povai. I am lucky to have had good people to help me.'

Not wanting to sound bitter, Hufrish reflected on the scenario for most players of her era. 'We would travel on our own. Do things on our own. Sometimes, I could use the family car within the city and do what I wanted. But not all were lucky. I would train in three phases – morning, afternoon, and sometimes starting at 9 p.m. I never had the perfect conditions. We would sleep on classroom desks in tournaments in some places, often held in schools. From outstation tournaments, we would return home in unserved coaches, sitting near the toilets. The prize was often blankets. They were different times. No cut-throat, no ill feelings towards fellow players.'

Hufrish's father played hockey and cricket in Dadar. She found support from her mother for playing badminton. 'My dad wanted me to study, and we could manage one sport. Studies and one sport was doable. Once I started doing well, winning tournaments, representing Maharashtra, and winning gold at a competition in Jaipur at twelve, I took badminton seriously, but I paid attention to my studies.'

She was never career oriented. 'Of course, I did my graduation and got a job at a bank (Union Bank). It would give me a half day off. Many years later, out of jealousy, one of the ex-players stopped me from leaving the office for badminton, and I opted for the voluntary retirement scheme because I wanted to do coaching. I didn't want a nine to five desk job.'

Remembering her good times, Hufrish spoke of her contemporaries. 'We saw a lot of good players from Malaysia and Indonesia. I was fascinated by players like Sumirat, Rudy Hartono (when I trained in Indonesia) and Fleming Delf. Morten Frost. Morten is a good friend. Susi Susantha was so good. Watching them, you learnt so much.'

Most Asian players were good at training, but the Europeans did all their practice on the court. They hit a thousand smashes and had three sets running six rounds of 400m. The Asians and the Europeans had different styles. Hartono was an exception. He skipped for one hour before the match.

Hufrish confessed that the Chinese were far superior. 'We didn't have their fitness. We could match the Chinese for the first seven points, and then they would take their game to the next level. They also played fearlessly. They were just too good. Maybe we didn't follow the right kind of training during the off-season. I would sometimes be at camps for nine months of year, but it didn't help me. My game would go down at the camps, and I was sick of the politics.'

Travelling overseas took a lot of effort when Hufrish was at her peak. 'We never went abroad like they do now – thrice a month. But I would go once every six months. In 1980, I went to the Uber Cup in Jakarta and stayed there for a few months. In 1985, I travelled to the UK to train with Tom John. He was also Vimal Kumar's coach. Those days, we were hardly allowed to go. I still managed to play a few tournaments.'

Going for one such tournament earned Hufrish the ire of the federation officials. 'When I went, there were repercussions for what I did because no one was allowed to do what we wanted. So when I returned with a contract from Slazenger, the chief coach did not like it. He dropped me from the team. I made a case against the BAI and won. But then, for the 1986 Asian Games, they did not even take me in the camp even though I was the fittest among the twelve members.'

Fazil Ahmed was the BAI president when Hufrish was granted a trial at Patiala. They had another camp in Bangalore. 'I beat everyone except Madhumita (Bisht) and Ami (Ghia). The BAI secretary accused me of spoiling the team's spirit. I was outspoken, but I fought for other players and suffered in the process.'

They could not stop her, and she got into the 1986 team on merit. Then she had an injury, even though Hufrish played until 1993. 'I had a slipped disc and did not get the stability in my knee. I had to cut down on my play. No one supported me in my case against the BAI except Madhumita.'

There are stories about her temper. 'Yes, I was very short-tempered, which sometimes would hurt me.' She lost finals in two senior and two junior championships. Ironically, she lost to Radhika Bose only once, in the final in 1981 at Gandhinagar. Before the final match, Hufrish received a strange message from the federation that if she lost the game, she would have to compete with the third-place finisher to qualify for selection for the All-England Championship.

'It was unheard of. I was distraught. I could not concentrate and lost. Fazil Ahmed was sitting on the sidelines. I could not take it at all. I hit the shuttle into his face and gave up that match. They spoiled so many careers. Mine was not the only one.' A couple of months after losing the final, Hufrish beat Radhika hands down in a tournament.

Hufrish had many friends from the fraternity and remembered them. 'I knew Meena, though I had never watched her play. Damayanti is a close friend of mine. She was the coach in the 1982 Asian Games. Her backhand and footwork were phenomenal. Sometimes, she would play with us when she was coaching. She was dexterous.

Damayanti would tell me that Meena, for her bulk, moved very well. Good anticipation. She was swift.'

The legendary Suresh Goel was one of her favourites. 'I partnered with Goel, too, once. His stroke play was so good. He had a fantastic temperament. His strokes were exceptional. I saw him once beat a junior player one-sided. I will always remember that one match that I played with him. He said, "Beti (daughter), just stand in front. I will take the backcourt." The best thing about him was he was very gentle and encouraging.'

Hufrish immersed herself in her coaching, which kept her in touch with badminton at the highest level. She travelled with the juniors and seniors of the Indian team and was understandably happy. 'I just love going to the badminton court every day. It is my bread and butter. It is my life.'

For Hufrish and Jwala Gutta, badminton may seem strange now, since a youngster participating in the game has the best facilities and federation support. They continue to serve badminton in their way, Hufrish, with her involvement with juniors at the CCI and Jwala at her academy. Their contribution has enriched Indian badminton. Jwala and Hufrish deserve greater recognition for standing up for their rights as players. They have suffered for speaking the truth.

13

Leroy D'Sa: The Steadfast Support

LOVE FOR PLAYING, FOR getting an opportunity to be outside one's home and play, is how a sportsperson in the making is likely to be introduced to the world of sports. Finding a patch of land to hit a six or score a goal would be the first step in making a few new friends. Conveying who their current favourite Bollywood star or cricketer is would help strike a bond and ensure the band turns up daily. The sport, which is already popular among older boys and grown-ups, stays integral to the group and finds its place in the hearts of newcomers. Sometimes, it doesn't and pushes one to look beyond their vicinity to satisfy their hunger for playing a sport. That's what happened to some of us and maybe that friend from the neighbourhood who one would find in the field every day on time but later would have found their calling in a different profession. That initial stepping stone is critical and eases one's journey to find a firm footing. It gives one a reason to look forward to the evening sessions, a perfect way to bring the day to a close after those gruelling hours in the classroom.

A similar tale finds a storyteller named Leroy Francis D'Sa. He was a doubles specialist who emerged in the early 1970s and was a prominent player through the 1980s. Leroy's feats at the 1982 Asian Games were exemplary – he won the doubles bronze with Pradeep Gandhe, the mixed doubles bronze with Kanwal, and the men's team bronze.

Leroy is the only Indian to have won three medals in the same edition of the Asian Games. Four years later, at the Seoul Asian Games, he added a bronze from the men's team to his collection. He also has a silver medal from the men's team event of the 1983 Asian Championships, held in Calcutta.

'Gandhe was a good partner to have. He managed to control the game's weaker parts and convert them into strengths. Gandhe was a thoughtful player; he covered different parts of the court while defending during rallies,' revealed Sanjay Sharma.

Leroy found his interest in badminton by casually experimenting with cricket, football, table tennis and even hockey. He lived in the Reserve Bank colony of Mumbai, where there was no dearth of facilities. The colony included a cricket pitch, a section for table tennis and a badminton court. With those options laid out, the choice to pick one is also tied to the cycle of seasons.

Rain might strip away all the friction required to land the perfect kick. Still, in return, it offers unforgettable memories. Leroy dabbled in football when it poured from above. He studied at St Mary's High School, where the culture of sports further brewed Leroy's interest. It inculcated in him a sense of love and respect towards all sports. He was selected for the cricket team because of his keen eye and good arm. His evenings post-school included playing an outdoor sport. As the sun bade goodbye for the day, he and his friends would settle in a badminton court or a table tennis arena. With athleticism already running in his genes, the exposure helped him hone his skills in every field of play.

When he was in the seventh standard, his father received a work transfer, and the family shifted to Hyderabad. Right after joining a school in the city of Nawabs, a badminton competition took place. Leroy performed well, and one of the coaches couldn't help but notice his craft in the sport. The teacher was so impressed that Leroy was offered to practise with a group of badminton aficionados. This paved his way into the school team, marking the start of what would go on to be a successful career in badminton.

His father, who had hockey experience, suggested that Leroy pick an individual sport. Leroy realised this without even a hint of a second thought. Destiny was already forging a path for him. 'Some players need a robust sport like football or hockey to excel, and some do well in individual sports.' This is combined with recognition for his gameplay right when he started. Leroy emphasises that the sport was indeed a matter of choice for him. Proving to be one of the few Christians who chose a sport aside from football and hockey, he fares among George Lewis, Roger Binny and others.

Leroy stepped away from the norm and made the best of the guidance and opportunities surrounding him to realise where his potential could mature into success. 'You will never find a Christian from Goa or Mangalore playing cricket. One or two madcaps would be seen here and there. An exception would be Roger Binny, but he too must have excelled in track and field, which was evident when I used to watch him go for his run-up while bowling,' Leroy recalls Roger Binny's stint in Javelin throw during his college days before he found his footing in the world of cricket.

Watching the masters of the game was a privilege that Leroy had. Back in the Reserve Bank colony of Bombay, several badminton tournaments were hosted, and they used to welcome many guest players. One of them was Natekar. Like his contemporaries, Leroy imbibed many of his initial badminton lessons and ethics by watching the sport in its amateur form, which is seen abundantly in local games. It helped him understand how the game was to be played more than how it was already being played.

Prakash Nath
Courtesy: Ratna Nath

Four-time national champion
Trilok Nath Seth
Courtesy: Shirish Nadkarni

Meena Shah
Courtesy: Shirish Nadkarni

Sushila Rege
Courtesy: Shirish Nadkarni

Nandu Natekar
Courtesy: The Hindu

Suresh Goel
Courtesy: The Hindu

Ami Ghia (front row, centre) *and*
Kanwal Thakar Singh (second row, centre) *on an overseas tour*
Courtesy: Shirish Nadkarni

Dinesh Khanna with the 1965 Asian Badminton Confederation (ABC) trophy; his recent portrait
Courtesy: Dinesh Khanna

Thomas Cup stalwarts: (clockwise from top left) *Dipu Ghosh, C.D. Deoras, Dinesh Khanna, Romen Ghosh, T.N. Seth, S.R. Chadha (manager) and Nandu Natekar*
Courtesy: Shirish Nadkarni

Flt Lt Vijay Tambay and Damayanti Tambay
Courtesy: Shirish Nadkarni

Damayanti Tambay with Prime Minister Lal Bahadur Shastri
Courtesy: Damayanti Tambay

Tara and Sunder Deodhar
Courtesy: Shirish Nadkarni

S.M. Arif
Courtesy: V.V. Subrahmanyam

Prakash Padukone and Pullela Gopi Chand
Courtesy: Badminton Association of India (BAI)

(Left to right) Vikram Bisht, Uday Pawar and Syed Modi
Courtesy: Madhumita Bisht

Ami Ghia, Kanwal Thakar Singh and Ameeta Singh with the Indian badminton team
Courtesy: Ami Ghia

(Top row, second from left) *Syed Modi*,
(sitting from extreme right) *Ami Ghia, Madhumita Bisht and Ameeta Singh and other members of the Indian badminton team*
Courtesy: Madhumita Bisht

Ameeta Singh and Manjusha Kanwar
From Vijay Lokapally's personal collection

Ami Ghia
Courtesy: Shirish Nadkarni

Ami Ghia with Shobha Moorthy (extreme left) *and Asif Parpia* (right)
Courtesy: Shirish Nadkarni

Satwiksairaj Rankireddy
Courtesy: BAI

Hufrish Nariman

Syed Modi and Prakash Padukone
Courtesy: Shirish Nadkarni

Madhumita Bisht
Courtesy: Shirish Nadkarni

Leroy D'Sa

(Left to right) *Vimal Kumar, Madhumita Bisht and Pullela Gopi Chand*
Courtesy: Madhumita Bisht

Srikanth Kidambi (left) *with his mentor Pullela Gopi Chand*
Courtesy: V.V. Subrahmanyam

H.S. Prannoy, Srikanth Kidambi and B. Sai Praneeth
Courtesy: V.V. Subrahmanyam

Aparna Popat with Prakash Padukone and coach Anil Pradhan
Courtesy: Shirish Nadkarni

Aparna Popat and Carolina Marin
Courtesy: Aparna Popat

Jwala Gutta and S.M. Arif
Courtesy: V.V. Subrahmanyam

Ashwini Ponnappa
Courtesy: BAI

Saina Nehwal
Courtesy: BAI

P.V. Sindhu
Courtesy: Qamar Sibtain

Bengaluru Raptors – Winner of the 2020 Premier Badminton League
Courtesy: Sportstar

Delhi Acers – Winner of the 2016 Premier Badminton League
Courtesy: Sportstar

Malvinder Dhillon with Manjusha Kanwar
From Vijay Lokapally's personal collection

Ajay Kanwar and P.V. Sindhu
Courtesy: Ajay Kanwar

The Indian team for the 1982 Asian Games: (from left) *coach Dipu Ghosh, Uday Pawar, Prakash Padukone, Syed Modi, Sanjay Sharma, Pradeep Gandhe and Partho Ganguly*
Courtesy: Shirish Nadkarni

Akshay Lokapally with badminton legend Nandu Natekar

It was only a short time until he returned to Bombay to further his badminton career.

He crossed the Juniors and immediately joined the Railways team. His first partner was Suresh Goel, acknowledged as the coach who imparted the most valuable lessons and as someone who saw a friend in Leroy. Coaching was almost unheard of, and training camps were not of the same quality as today, so these tips were invaluable for Leroy. 'Maybe a few years later we would have people from now reminiscing how things were harder during their prime, or maybe history will repeat itself, and things will go back to the simplicity of the 1970s and 1980s,' Leroy expresses his more profound thoughts unhesitatingly. His remark on the possibility of a future where we feel the need to return to specific practices of older times is thought-provoking. It speaks of those aspects of today which can find inspiration from the past.

Leroy, even today, feels that he was fortunate to have played in an era where watching seniors in action was an option. In 1973, 76 and 77, he partnered Padukone to win the National doubles. His partner in 1975 was Suresh Goel. He was joined by Sanat Misra in 1983, 84 and 86. For variety, he won the mixed doubles with Amia Ghia, making him arguably the best doubles player in India's badminton history. Sanat had the strength to connect with his partners. He and Leroy were a good combination.

'Leroy was a phenomenal doubles player. He and Goel made a fabulous combination and his pairing with Misra was remarkable too. In doubles, his service was flawless and his net-play was very strong. He was able to control the net so well by pushing the shuttle into the opponent's body and the return from the other end would be feeble, high in the air, which helped Goel in going for a powerful smash. Suresh had a lovely smash on both flanks,' recalls Shirish Nadkarni.

Bombay had a terrific badminton culture. It had a circuit of 12–13 local tournaments every year. Every Gymkhana used to hold an annual tournament. To start from the Vanita Samaj in the middle of June, then you go to Bhagini Samaj, CCI, Central Railway Institute, Khar Gymkhana, Bombay Gymkhana and Sachivalaya Gymkhana. So, if they were good enough, every player who hoped to excel at the game used to play all these tournaments, including all events like singles, doubles, and mixed doubles.

'This culture had existed for many years. It was there through my youth but unfortunately died away at the turn of the century. Ami, Aparna and six times state champion Gautam Thakkar were Gujjus, Atul Premnarayan was from Punjab, Anil Pradhan was a Maharashtrian. So, people from different regions and castes of India thrived in the bustling culture of Bombay. For almost twenty years, it had vanished. About 3–4 years ago, it started to come back. I hope Bombay's badminton culture will be back,' laments Nadkarni. It was out of necessity as there were no better ways of learning or maybe it was a characteristic of the time. Still, it gave an advantage that wasn't offered by other means. Since some tournaments – including the Nationals – were held with senior and junior divisions competing in the same arena, the juniors had the liberty to learn and then emulate the play style of the senior contenders. He wasn't treated like a junior when he was promoted to the senior division. Suresh would treat him equally, which helped Leroy adapt and settle faster in the new environment. He also gave him an important lesson.

With the Indonesian game dominating international badminton, which would later face stiff competition from China, both displayed a style embellished by swift movements and various jumps. 'Leroy, does the shuttle not return to the ground after it has been tossed? Do you think it is necessary to jump?' Leroy recalls this quip made by

Suresh to teach him the differences in body structure and the fitness level of Indian players at that time. Suresh knew the advantages of a jump, the time it can shave off, which could likely result in the opponent missing the shuttle by an inch after a protracted stretch of all the limbs. But he was aware of the fitness levels of Indian players, and so instead, he pushed the youngsters to play to their strengths.

He recalls that in those days, players were allowed to travel in reserved seats on trains only on their way to tournaments. Otherwise, they always travelled in the unreserved category, even on the way back home from a tournament. Sometimes they had to sit in a corner of the aisle or near the toilet. 'While returning from the 1982 Asian Games, I was sitting outside the bathroom of the first-class compartment with my bronze medal,' he complains, claiming that he still finds it hard to forget the stench. 'Today, it's way more professional. If a player exits a tournament, they take the first flight out of the city. In our time, if we had lost on a Friday, we would have still remained to watch the remaining rounds, especially the final on Sunday. Then we would have taken a train home on Monday,' Leroy takes a hard look at the relationships in the current badminton world. There was everlasting camaraderie between players back then. Nonetheless, they also saw each other as enemies on the court, reflecting no dearth of competition.

Televisions had just started finding a spot on tables most commonly found in Indian drawing rooms with a floral tablecloth or even an old bed sheet on top, so they weren't as common. And the absence of mobile phones meant the only pastime was reading. Before leaving for national camps, Leroy would ensure his suitcase had enough space for at least 10–12 books. But this would mean only some of his free time was devoted to reading books. During camps, he and all the other players would travel to town to catch a movie.

In Bangalore, Sundays were reserved for visiting a local eatery around Brigade Road, serving juicy steaks and desserts. In Patiala, butter chicken would pique his olfactory senses and make him gather everyone for an evening outside. He hated wasting food, so he ensured he was always surrounded by girls. 'Their eyes were bigger than their stomachs, and I was a big foodie' his eyes gleam with the memories of Hufrish not being able to finish everything on her plate on multiple occasions and like a hawk, Leroy somehow was always around to polish off the remains.

Such stories are only created when there is a genuine fondness for each other. Indeed, everyone wanted to best the other. But, to do so, they would never even think of putting hurdles in each other's way. Feeling bad for oneself over a defeat was only natural, but it was never followed by episodes of bitching. 'I don't see that now. I have noticed players today stay in groups, one group here or one group there. There were no groups during our time,' Leroy remarks.

Leroy practised most of the time with the female lot. He credits a significant chunk of his lessons to Ami and Hufrish, his sparring partners. Ami was soft and deceptive, and Hufrish was rough. Playing with them made him realise his protective nature, which he notably displayed towards them. He would ensure they received enough training by the end of the day. Leroy played a lot of mixed doubles with Kanwal, nicknamed 'babbu'.

Leroy enjoyed playing with her as she had a sense of humour that pleased Leroy. When it came to the boys at the camps, they all had each other's backs. If Uday Pawar wanted to practice a particular stroke, he would request Leroy to stay back and vice versa. Partho Ganguly and former player Vikram Bisht shared the same sentiment. They would all wait for each other even though their share of practice was over for the day. 'We didn't know much about what all to do, but whatever we did, we ensured that each among us did the same as well,' said Leroy. Partho was a fit and agile player, both in singles and doubles. He enjoyed a long career.

Leroy started his badminton career by playing singles, like many others. And he enjoyed being the only one on his side of the court. But destiny had a few other plans. At the junior level, he figured it was getting increasingly complex for him to sustain the required performance levels to compete against the likes of Padukone. 'Prakash had a huge influence on me. I would like to have emulated him, but unfortunately, too many distractions came my way,' admits Leroy. He confesses to having known all the game patterns like Padukone did. It was Padukone's sagacity that led him to the stardom that he's known for. In his last year, Leroy made the switch.

'Leroy's advantage was that he only played doubles and was always well rested. He is one of the best doubles players from our time,' praised Pawar.

It was a stride that brought fame to his name and a kickstart to India's doubles journey. He doesn't shy away from talking about his regrets. In fact, he openly expresses to them that he hopes some youngster is imbued with the same lesson that he understood years later. He knew singles needed extra work, but Leroy was an outgoing, happy-go-lucky type. His fervour for badminton was matched by his desire to party on Saturdays and spend some carefree time with friends.

'One cigarette and drink would become several in no time,' confesses Leroy, who claims that his stamina was not impacted by his indiscretions. 'I can't recall a situation where I lost a match because I was tired,' he said defiantly. 'I lost because I didn't play well, or my opponent was better.' But he admits that all the excesses took a toll on his ability to focus. It creeps slowly into the brain like a worm until it shows itself abruptly. He believes he wouldn't have lost many crucial matches if his focus was unshaken.

'Leroy was a bit podgy during his growing years. He became slimmer in the subsequent years. He would have been even more effective if he was slimmer from early on. His gameplay was strong in the mid-court and at the net fortified by his defence but wasn't as effective from the back,' comments Nadkarni. Leroy lacked a strong smash whose thunder surfs on the echoes inside a closed hall. Body type, shape and size mattered a lot surely in sport like badminton which demands a lot of athleticism, as realised by a handful of champions, if not all, about themselves.

Today, when Leroy imparts the same knowledge to his students, he tells them that it comes from someone who has first-hand experience of what he is talking about and knows what it means to have regrets. He firmly believes it is better to learn such lessons from him instead of Prakash, who did not indulge in such distractions. He wishes someone bold in his life too at that time had denounced his actions. Parents were mostly unaware since most of it would be outside the house. Considering Leroy's stature and outspoken and loud persona, he feels his friends would have hesitated to approach and guide him.

A friend once told him, 'You are a very talented player, and so you are lazy.' Leroy feels his friend should have told him he didn't play to his full potential. He believes if he had put in even 50 per cent of the effort Prakash used to, he might have succeeded in singles. He knew his fitness was not up to the mark to play singles – but to improve it demanded more work, meaning he would have to give up his fun time. It was not a sacrifice that he was willing to make. Today, Leroy doesn't allow hesitation to get in the way. He is frank with his trainees whenever such a conversation is needed.

Leroy likes to highlight his prowess at singles during his early years. Once, in an inter-Railways tournament he beat players who were part of the Indian Railways singles team despite having not played singles for seven to eight years. However, his complacency with his fitness meant that he had to say goodbye to a professional career in singles. He saw this as a chance to achieve fame in an unexplored territory. Leroy made the switch to play only doubles and began his journey as a doubles specialist. It was a step that would bring him fame. And that's how he began his journey as a doubles specialist.

Leroy's game was versatile, and he could smoothly adapt to playing doubles. His knowledge of table tennis helped him see badminton through a different lens, and he developed a new concept of defence that he called 'back and counter'. He even coached many of the sport's stalwarts hailing from Hyderabad, such as Dilip Raj Saxena, Mir Khasim Ali and N. V. Ashok. He was successful with this new approach. When other players watched him play the shot with confidence, they started imitating and even improving on the technique. Leroy stopped playing defence with his forehand after that. He had a strong hand-eye coordination that made him unfailing at the net. The opposition team had to keep their defence high or hit the shuttle to the back of the court because a flat return would mean a ruthless interception by Leroy.

Unfortunately for Leroy, most of his peers did not prioritise doubles despite the prestige the category had internationally. In fact, nations such as Indonesia and Malaysia nurtured players who would exclusively play doubles. An elite player like Christian Hadinata, known for his doubles supremacy, was a one-time All-England finalist in singles. Park Joo-Bong, who treated Hadinata as his idol, is considered one of the best doubles players by many. Park was also a singles player and occasionally medalled in singles. After switching from singles, they devoted all their focus to the doubles event. Other players who also played doubles were Thomas Kihlstrom, Rudy Hartono, Liem Swie King and the Danish players.

Even though they found it different from singles for obvious reasons, it brought them immense recognition, success and satisfaction. In India, players wanted to make their way into the team through singles, knowing the doubles standard was inferior. But today, we see the choice being made right at the junior stage. Some players focus solely on mixed doubles, and husband–wife pairs are not a rare sight. Our associations and training centres adapted to the change in the later stages, a move that was absent in Leroy's time. Indeed, Padukone and P. Gopi Chand were exceptions and played doubles.

According to Leroy, training camps began to take hold in India only after the Asian Games were held in the country in 1982. It was the first time Indian players enjoyed playing with imported shuttlecocks. Otherwise, they used to play and practice with Garuda shuttlecocks. 'Though there were camps at regular intervals, each six to eight weeks long with breaks in between, it was mostly a self-made endeavour. Our coaches were present, but we didn't have any sort of specialised coaching,' said Leroy.

As the saying goes, all good things come to an end – the gifts that the Asian Games brought were soon taken away. There was no follow-up once Asiad ended. Players thought they could manage independently, but that was difficult. Only after Padukone's victory in the 1980 All-England, when he started his academy and courts after returning to India, did we see a system where deserving players got an opportunity to learn and grow. He had sown the seeds for the future.

'They didn't care to follow up,' Leroy said with a lot of indignation in his heart. The same level of heed was not paid after what the players had witnessed before and during Asiad. Highlighting the example of China, he emphasised that their national chief coach and his deputy travel around the large country to instruct and oversee the proper functioning of the various regional centres.

China's success at the sport confirms the importance of having a proper coaching infrastructure. Leroy feels that his career would have been different if that knowledge and expertise were available back then. He points out that the mistakes he made along with his partner in the doubles matches at the Asian Games were unknowingly repeated in the team event as well, something which could have been avoided if a coach had been observing their games. This might have led to a silver or gold medal instead of the bronze they ended up with.

Leroy refuses to say that doubles were subjected to stepmotherly treatment since, in his eyes, it was more akin to being an orphan. The only notable medals in doubles were from the 1982 Asiad. With a lack of foresight on the path that doubles could take, Leroy unflinchingly admits that India needed a stronger doubles team. Padukone's gold in All-England saw a newfound confidence emerge in both professional players and the aficionado trying their best.

It would take many years – twenty-one to be precise – to secure another gold medal in the reputed tournament and the same event by Gopi Chand. Asia had a few international tournaments of the same calibre as the important ones in the European circuit such as Denmark Open, Scandinavian Open, Dutch Open and All-England. These were usually preceded by the nationals.

Leroy convincingly believes that their game was not inferior as it was made out to be by many at the time. Of course, Prakash's performance and achievements commanded the badminton fraternity's respect. Still, there were few opportunities for the rest to improve. 'Go back to your stable and relearn,' Leroy recalls a saying. But there was no way to do so. They mainly learnt by trial and error.

The question of how a player could survive at a time when sponsorships were limited and prize money evasive cannot be ignored.

Leroy openly admits how lucky he was to have had employment while playing. It helped players like him remain financially secure and independent, even though it meant fewer hours to practice. They had to mandatorily put in a certain number of hours at work, but they would be allowed a half-day from time to time. He and others trying to balance work and play had to ensure the availability of courts during the other half of the day to make the best use of the leave. This strain never deterred him; it only fuelled him even more to pursue his love for the sport.

He believes that easily available sporting facilities are essential to develop the players of tomorrow. 'When two people have a decent court to play on and enough shuttlecocks are available, they will learn the sport just by playing and practising it,' he said, highlighting the importance of infrastructure over coaches. He thinks that the television coverage sports have today has made it possible to learn a sport simply by watching it on a screen. However, he laments that most courts in Mumbai are for recreational badminton rather than competitive play.

All coaching at the Prakash Academy or at the Gopi Chand Academy is professionally done. Every muscle in your body is exercised. They have so many hours of exercise and practice, all done in a professional manner. That is why we have come up to the standards of the international players. 'But if you go to China, they have a different system. Li Yongbo, who was their national coach for several years, has done 'torture training' for all those years, including with Lin Dan. And that is why they achieved great heights. From 2000 to 2010 and 2010 to 2018, China was on top. Once they were welcomed back into the folds of the International

Badminton Federation in 1981, their women dominated,' Nadkarni pointed out.

Speaking of the current format, which is twenty-one points, Nadkarni observes it favours the underdog. Earlier, you could only win a point on service. You had a player like Abhinshyam Gupta, who was a defensive player. 'He was so steady that he hardly conceded a negative point. So, he would play against somebody for almost one hour. And still, the match score would be dangling around 15–2, 15–3 because the service used to change hands so many times. Now if it changes hands six times, it will be 3–3, the score is moving forward. You can have a maximum of 59 rallies during a match because the maximum score can be 30–29.'

Leroy is a famous coach at the P. J. Hindu Gymkhana in Mumbai. Still obsessed with badminton, Leroy finds that he can't stay away from the game. Individuals like him have made a relatively unnoticed but significant contribution to the progress of badminton in India. He is thrilled at the doubles success of young Indian players like Satwik and Chirag Shetty. They are carrying on the tradition of Leroy and others who specialised in doubles, two bodies playing with one mind on the court.

14

Manjusha Kanwar: Conquering Courts with Courage

SHE WAS HAPPY TO be a tomboy for many reasons. It gave her a sense of security. She could step out of the house with confidence. Due to the prevalent circumstances, it was a choice thrust upon Manjusha Kanwar, née Pawangadkar. Coming from Pune, a city as progressive as any in the country, Manjusha did not have the kind of fear that girls had in many cities of India. Pune girls have always kept pace with time, and she was all the more receptive to competing to have a decent life.

She got her early lessons growing up in Zambia. 'My parents, brother and entire family were playing club-level badminton,' she recalled. Manjusha returned to India at thirteen and began a stint in swimming. She was good at it, but essentially, she wanted to put on muscle by swimming because she was skinny. 'My legs were like matchsticks.' Her coach, Mr Rawat, who had trained Deepti Thanekar, initially rejected Manjusha. 'She can't play badminton,' he had declared. Manjusha was considered too thin and needed more power to pursue badminton at a competitive level. She was told that badminton was the wrong sport for her. Those words from the coach galvanised her into taking badminton seriously. He had thrown a challenge, and Manjusha accepted it.

To Manjusha's fortune, there was another coach, Mr Gore. 'He was my godfather. I was not a conventional player but willing to work hard. I was a dreamer.'

Manjusha's lessons in badminton now came on a cemented court. It helped her immensely when Mr Gore admitted her into his academy. He guided her in studies and badminton, driving Manjusha around on his scooter. 'I was not at all strong. My wrist movement was the key. I had sharp strokes.' It was tough for her opponents as she moved her wrist to fox them.

Manjusha, however, lost to Archana Deodhar fifteen times in a row on the local circuit. Her parents thought it was over for Manjusha, but the turning point came at the age of eighteen when she won her first junior and senior tournament titles in Mumbai. She beat Seema Bhandari in the seniors and Archana in the juniors. 'My father then sat me down and allowed me to play full-time badminton.'

Full-time sports meant that studies took a back seat because she had to attend camps. Here, state badminton player Uday Pawar was a considerable influence. His reading of the game was great. Manjusha's knee was operated on twice, and every time she returned to the courts, Pawar made her play in all the categories. 'I am what I am because of Mr Gore. He gave me early hope and direction for my career and life. Any youngster needs such support, and I am glad I got one.'

It was not easy for Manjusha to learn lessons because there was no television in her formative years to follow badminton worldwide. Only after she played in international tournaments did she start imitating the Chinese star Ye Zou Hin. Manjusha was stunned by her tremendous reverse drop and how she cut the shuttle. 'I had a bad badminton body. My right leg was inverted, and no one guided me. I could not lunge and, a few times ended up spraining my ankle. No one corrected me. With these limitations, I could not make a big mark at the international level.' Surprisingly, no coach spotted it. Manjusha was good with half-smashes and always went for the lines.

The 1994 National Championships paved the way for Manjusha to approach the Padukone Academy. The experience was fruitful, and she admitted, 'I was aware of my limitations. They put me through rigorous strength training, and I just collapsed.' She left the academy because she could not cope with the rigorous training. She lost the national title to P. V. V. Lakshmi in 1994 but returned strongly to regain it in 1996. 'Prakash sir was surprised and said, 'I did not see these half-smashes in Bangalore.'

P. V. V. Lakshmi won against Manjusha in two straight games with a score of 12–9 and 11–6. She paused Manjusha's streak of national titles, as this could have been her fourth. Then Chief Minister of Punjab, Mr Beant Singh, magnanimously offered a sum of ₹1 lakh each to Lakshmi and Dipankar Bhattacharjee, who won the men's singles title. Considering this was during the mid-1990s and a non-international sporting event – though it was a prestigious one – the sum was quite generous for its time.

Manjusha remembers her interactions with Padukone as life lessons. 'Padukone's lecture, in which he emphasised hard work and old-school thought, was so impactful. He always said, 'You have to work, make no complaints, and make the most of what you have.'

Manjusha observed that money was not everything for her generation. It is different now. 'They know how to encash and enjoy leagues to earn money.' The approach remains the same: hard work can't be substituted. 'In our era, we felt proud of having played for India. Representing the country was not enough – we also understood we had to make some money. Sadly, some of us took the defeats to heart.'

She was part of a system that was responsible for managing the workload on the players themselves. Each player had a unique style of training. During national camps, players were put under pressure to adapt and improve. 'I never enjoyed running. Instead, I used swimming to increase my lung capacity. I relied on playing kho-kho and kabaddi to enhance my flexibility. I only practised shadowing.'

Manjusha could not do strength training and preferred to play in three sessions in a day. 'In my era, coaches couldn't tell you what you were supposed to do.' She would be up at 5:30 a.m. seven days a week to concentrate on speed by playing and learning to outpace her opponent. Her game was deceptive. Often, her opponents could not anticipate her movements because she was not aggressive in her approach.

Manjusha, self-admittedly, was not a flexible player. She could not touch her toes. Could not lift weights. She, however, had great energy. 'I would never be tired. It was more mental than physical.' Sometime in 1992, she had a session with a Chinese coach. She would look to escape weight training because her body would hurt. When it came to the 400-metre dash, she would beat everybody. She was a fast runner, and that's the reason she had the on-court endurance to last.

In Manjusha's case, it had a lot to do with her mental strength. Her warm-up was to keep moving the wrist. Only a few girls were able to move their wrists like Manjusha. Her half-smashes came in handy against short players. The primary factor that worked for Manjusha was her footwork. She strove to stay in the 50 to 53 kg bracket. One more kilogram and she would struggle on the court. 'My timing helped me the most since I lacked conventional footwork. I never liked strength training because my body would hurt.' She derived strength from meditation and vowing never to complain.

The tomboy image helped Manjusha to train with the boys. She took the help of the marker (Babu Rao), collected her shuttles and got down to play with the boys.

'I liked my space. They would throw shuttles. These markers helped me a lot. I never showed my fatigue even though I was in pain.' Swimming helped her fight arthritis. She also sought refuge in classical music and the band Carpenters and Abba.

Ami complimented her in 1989 when she won the CCI junior and senior titles. 'I had hardly done any training at the 40-day camp. I was so happy to have won. I was busy playing with the boys because no one concentrated on me. I was seventeen. Archana was a superb player. I lost two junior finals to her. In doubles, I would run and had to move a lot on the court. That helped me improve my game.'

When Manjusha was at the top, Dipankar Bhattacharjee was dominating the national scene. 'He was brilliant.' She observed him and tried to imbibe his aggression. But most of the girls were not willing to work hard. Manjusha would toil for hours on the court, but sadly, she did not have the backing of the federation to be sent to overseas tournaments. Shuttle speed would vary when playing in tournaments abroad, and many, like Manjusha, needed to handle those challenges better.

For her, singles remained the main thing. The federation was sending Gopi Chand and Madhumita more frequently. Manjusha needed more sponsors. 'I had to buy my shuttles. I would buy shuttles whenever I went abroad. Dribbling with new shuttles was not known, but at tournaments in India, I would collect shuttles for practice. We would have a box of shuttles, and they were like a gold mine.' Gopi Chand, she recalled, was the golden boy of Indian badminton and never faced a shortage of shuttles because he would win tournaments and invest the prize money in buying shuttles.

In later years, Manjusha tried to educate parents who wanted their daughters to pursue sports careers.

'I remember saying at a lecture that you have to think twice before wanting your child to play sports as a professional career.' There were issues when travelling alone. In her case, she would purposely dress up like a boy and keep her hair short. 'I wanted to look like a boy. I did not want to attract attention. There were times when people mistook me for a boy. That was my defence mechanism.' She was an extrovert in her own way. She looked to win prize money tournaments to meet expenses for staying alone because 'I was not comfortable sharing rooms.'

Manjusha played eight finals in the nationals and lost three of them. 'I should not have lost to some opponents – losing to Aparna (Popat) at Hyderabad was losing to a good opponent. She played well, but I could have won more tournaments if I had been smarter.' The problem was Manjusha could not express herself. The badminton court was her life. 'It was my temple, my home. I matured very late in my life.' Her career had many problems because she could not make the right decisions at the right time.

There were many qualities of Manjusha's peers which would have propelled her to do better. She started late and needed to watch seniors more to learn. She, however, gained a lot from the boys' support system. 'They accommodated me well. I could be myself.' There was rivalry between the girls, and they did not appreciate that Manjusha was with the boys. 'I watched a lot of Gopi, Uday Pawar, Rajeev Bagga, Dipankar. I owe a lot to Uday. He knew my strengths and flaws.'

Sadly, on the national scene, she was not popular with the chief coach (T. P. Puri) and the federation. Puri had his favourites, and she was not the one who would touch the feet of the federation officials. 'I was not that type. That didn't benefit me long-term because they expected it from other players.'

How did she look at the feminine attributes of the players? Did they impact the game? 'Neelima was different. Like Jwala. But not many. Deepti Thanekar was very feminine, very gentle.' Manjusha knew India was a tough place to be in if you were a girl. You could not express yourself as a girl. The seniors would not allow you to do anything. So, she looked to beat them on the court. Off the court, she was like a sheep in their company. But on the court, Manjusha was a lioness because that was her domain. 'I would have done better with more self-belief. Unfortunately, I didn't know my own game at times.'

All the Uber Cups that Manjusha played in were perfect. She was crestfallen when they did not send her to the Asian and Commonwealth Games. 'My attacking game was my forte. French Open 2000, Aparna lost love and love in the final to an opponent I lost in three games, but Aparna was always very effective against the Europeans.' It hurt Manjusha. She needed to have that consistency because she was not strong on her feet.

Aparna played an effective game against the Europeans. Manjusha had wrist strength but not shoulder strength. 'I needed that strength the most. That's the only regret.' She could not improve her strength. She could not get the muscle in her game. For badminton, you had to have someone like Dipankar. 'He had explosive thighs and tremendous power. I would have made a mark if I had worked on my strengths. Not that I would have been an international champion.'

Manjusha was an underachiever despite her talent and hard work. 'I agree. I could have been much more.' Look at Aparna, for example. Her footwork was exceptional. She also gained from having a travelling coach. She was groomed well. When Manjusha beat her, it was to convey that it was not just about the academy. Madhumita and Aparna had the support. The coaches also backed them. 'I loved their game and their determination.'

Manjusha's best years were from 1991 to 1996 before Aparna arrived on the scene. Aparna was hailed as the upcoming sensation, silencing the critics and proving all the naysayers wrong. Aparna was not there when Manjusha was at her peak. 'I would not try to remember my rivalries. I always looked to move forward. I have forgotten many things. During those years, I was the fittest and strongest. I should have been playing overseas. I needed that Commonwealth Games in 1994. It did not happen, sadly.'

Manjusha also reflected on when coaches did not appreciate the girls indulging in cosmetic makeup. 'You could not express yourself as a woman. Also, it was not helpful when a coach ran us down, saying women in India can't win an international medal.' It was not gender specific. You had to do well to earn recognition.

Was there a time when the BAI did not want a mixed doubles event? Was it favouritism? Did personality make an impact? 'I don't think there was any discrimination. Women had to take a back seat, but in my time, it was favouritism. It was safer to go with men because they were the towering personalities of the game.'

The English were too dominant in mixed doubles, so men were given priority. In India, personal connections can impact results within the heavily outcome-based system. That matters. Women players needed help to make an impact in a men-dominated circuit. It was an arduous journey for women. 'In my time, we had Russians and Malaysians. We played a lot of matches. I have seen that part. It was good exposure. We should have had a lot more tournaments.' Times have changed now. Women players are not lagging. Saina and Sindhu are the leaders of the modern game.

Manjusha had a perfect backhand, but her forehand was weak; side movement was weak. Her defence was excellent because of the doubles and mixed doubles games that she played regularly. At the junior level, other countries make it a point to involve them in doubles. If a doubles player plays the singles, it helps. 'It is not easy. You will need to play all events at the junior level. You get your reflexes.' It helps a player improve the defence since the shuttle approaches you faster. 'We have a doubles coach now. Unheard of when I was playing.' Manjusha believed India could improve their doubles team by drafting strong players from the northeast, stating that the coach needed a broader pool to select from.

Manjusha followed a disciplined lifestyle. She would rise at 5:30 at the camps to be with nature. Finish her warm-up before starting the practice in the hall. 'They told me not to look into the mirror because trying to look good was considered a distraction.' The routine remained, and she was, remarkably, always on time. 'My life had a constant connection with badminton. My game was all about precision in the rectangle.'

Today's players are different. They hardly make self-assessments. 'They just want to be told by their coaches. They sit, and the coaches stand.' The players are reluctant to experiment, too, and are quick to blame the coach and the academy. Earlier, facilities were limited, and the players were self-driven. Wearing the national colours was a matter of pride. 'Representing India was a big thing.'

Manjusha only got to play international badminton a little despite ten national titles. 'When I got the chance, I got injured. Then, the 1990s were full of tough matches. The Danes were coming up. The Indonesians were dominating. The Koreans and the Chinese were always threatening to dominate the world stage. I mostly remember playing the Chinese. If you took a game off them, it would be considered good. I was playing All-England, Asian circuit, China Open. But they were too big for me.'

She laments the loss of camaraderie these days. There is too much bitterness. Players don't even talk to each other after the game is over. Manjusha notes, 'It was different in my time. We had strong friendships. We had groups, we were vocal, and we helped each other. Today, these gadgets have come as a disconnect. You don't need to speak to people.'

A negative effect of modern amenities is that service staff miss out on tips. Even to practise with someone, you must be friends. 'They are mostly on the phone when they should be speaking to fellow players. When I travel with the juniors today, I tell them to communicate.'

Assessing her contemporaries, Manjusha felt, 'Lakshmi was physically strong, Aparna had a good game, good net play. She was a disciplined, reticent player, never showed her anger, and never tried to cheat. We had mutual respect for our game. Jwala was very large-hearted. She transformed the doubles and mixed doubles with her attitude. She had a fantastic serve and return. I liked her. Very sweet. Very talented. She stood up to make her point. She spoke and tried to change the system for the next generation.'

Saina is her favourite. 'She is a once-in-a-lifetime player. She has changed the face of Indian badminton. I have the highest regard for her. My last tournament was her first. We shared a room. I have seen her grow. She has dedicated her life to badminton.'

Manjusha asserted that Saina was highly confident despite being treated poorly by some of her fellow players. 'However, she had the last laugh as Sindhu had the advantage of her father's support. On the other hand, Sindhu was mentally firm and worked hard, which helped her succeed. Despite all the fame, she remained grounded and was known to be lovely. Saina's growth gave her confidence and motivation to perform better.'

Manjusha emphasised that Saina and Sindhu were discovered over time. 'You had to punish your body to reach that level. The determination of a Jwala is much needed at the top. I have gained from my seniors and have tried passing on the experience, too.'

Manjusha, in her second phase as a badminton administrator, is convinced the times are best for the game. 'India of today is remarkable. I see it through my lens: the Sports Authority of India, the federation. It is a fantastic time to be a badminton player. The system has become so supportive. They will give you funds even at the lowest level. The Khelo India scheme is phenomenal.'

She is convinced that living in a metropolitan city is tough. 'It is not safe for a girl to travel alone. Metro cities can teach you business skills and technology but not in sports. Small towns teach you to be tough. Badminton has become an elite sport, and it is costly. You need sponsors and funding. If we can promote sports events in small cities, we can create more champions. It is a negative to pursue sports in metro cities where the facilities are expensive. I think badminton has become an elite sport.'

She believes that Chinese influence will wane. 'Badminton won't be Chinese dominated. The 21-point scoring opened the game and gave much-needed openings for the Indians.' Fitness was the key strength of the Chinese, so scoring points against them was tough. 'It can't get better than today. You can have a personal coach, trainer, physiotherapist, and psychologist. Sometimes, I feel badminton players are spoiled and have become complacent.'

For Manjusha, the 2004 edition was her last National Championship. A ten-time national champion (four singles, four doubles, two mixed doubles), her final Uber Cup was Saina's entry. They were room partners. It was also a signal for Manjusha to move on. The new order had arrived in the shape of Saina.

Settled in Delhi with husband Ajay and daughter Reva, Manjusha takes time off to visit Pune. 'There is a huge difference between the Pune of my teenage years and now. No one can get to Pune at my time. My parents did not worry because I had the best seniors: Hemant Hardikar, Ashwani Tawkar, and Meena Khade. All were family members. The bonding was amazing. I really could not have asked for more. Today's Pune is horrible. Times have changed so much.'

Manjusha is now busy at the Indian Oil office. The corporate structure keeps her on her toes as she plans policies for the sportspersons employed with Indian Oil. She also dedicates her time to laudable initiatives like carrying on reforms for jail inmates, teaching them badminton. Her connection with badminton remains strong. 'I would have been a swimmer if I had not played badminton.'

15

Madhumita Bisht: A Feathered Fury

MADHUMITA STARTED HER ILLUSTRIOUS journey in Siliguri, West Bengal. It has transformed into a metropolitan city now, but it was a small town back then. It is an important commercial and transportation hub because of Nathu La Pass, which passes through East Sikkim and facilitates trade with China. It gained prominence due to its proximity to Darjeeling's tea-producing hills. The British had control of those hills but needed a reliable transport system to get to them. They laid a narrow-gauge railway track and built the Siliguri Town railway station, connecting the scenic hills with the town. Siliguri has since been known for its tea. Expectedly, Madhumita, too, loves her tea.

She had the knack to quickly learn and adjust to the rhythm of all the different sports she played. She was an athlete as well as a volleyball player while in school. 'I was a better volleyball player when I started playing badminton, but my father convinced me to take up an individual sport,' she recalls. A parent's encouragement to pick an individual sport is not unheard of.

Those who are adept and athletic get to express their abilities the most when facing their opponent unhindered by the intricate dynamics of working with a partner or the lack of it. At that raw age, when muscles are gaining shape and nerves are ensuring that they do so, an individual sport helps one take ownership of one's defeat and welcome a victory.

Most sports have team events, and once such players establish themselves, the merits of a team game start unfolding. The lessons learnt from those are different but also consequential from what a solo journey might teach. Madhumita, too, found great mentors, stories and joy in those partnerships.

During the mid-seventies, Siliguri had no indoor badminton hall. The town was supposed to host an All-India Badminton Tournament, which seemed right out of a picturesque painting. The only way it could have been possible was by raising a giant tent on the premises of a college that would house the badminton courts, nurture the stars and give birth to some prodigies on the sidelines.

Two large wooden planks were placed together. Madhumita had a chance to visit the venue and remembers watching the play of Padukone, Devinder Ahuja, Partho Ganguly, Asif Parpia and others with immense interest. She was young then, but old enough to feed the embryonic passion and a desire to pursue the sport.

Her father was working as an exhibition officer. The family lived in a government colony quarter. In the neighbourhood lived a helpful gentleman, who was an ardent follower, as well as a player of badminton. A mud court stood in the middle of the colony that didn't offer the delights of a wooden court. Nonetheless, it satisfied their urge to toss around the shuttle in the evening. A state-level tournament was conducted on the same court when Madhumita was around seven or eight, which is enough evidence of the level of professional sport around her in her childhood.

Coming from Bengal, a state that celebrates its festivals with much enthusiasm, Madhumita remembers those memories of the tournament with the same celebratory zeal that finds incarnation in all Bengalis during the revered Durga Pujo. She used to pick a plastic bat and play her badminton around the court, a jamboree in itself, as she recalls.

Around 1975, names like Sudha Bafna, Suchita Abhyankar, Tulsidas and Anuradha Sarkar used to appear in the All-India Badminton Tournament. Because of the few names in the girls' category, the organisers put Madhumita's name on the roster. The Baghajatin Club used to hold the tournament. She didn't even have a racquet, but her father encouraged her and made sure she went and played. He never let himself or the family bend to customary norms.

Madhumita went and played her first game against Sudha, who pummelled her in a blunt game. Madhumita might have scored a point at best. But that didn't dampen her spirits. Her father had raised her to remember a mantra that would be helpful in any situation she lands herself in: if she plays against a tall player, then a win or a loss doesn't matter, and if she manages to score even a single point, then it is a victory in itself that she should be proud of. Some would disagree with this psychology. Still, it helped to assuage any disappointment in the young child's heart and infused an attitude to go and snatch the point that belonged to her, and then the next one and so on.

Madhumita started playing in more tournaments in Calcutta, as well as Malda, which was a town that had bloomed into a city. Matches were held on mud courts at some of the venues. Madhumita readily agreed to the slightest persuasion from her father to appear in those tournaments. The Siliguri All-India Invitation Tournament was an annual event but a definite one.

Then, there was also a Darjeeling Tournament to adorn the land, which shimmered with pristine air. On all these occasions, she would land at the venue with her father much before the assigned time to spot the best players and watch their game. Learning warming-up techniques, different grips used by them and understanding the right time for every stroke. Watching other performers and learning what to absorb in one's game through trial and error distinguished a star from a regular player. With few options at one's disposal, one had to develop an eagle eye.

There was no one to explain to her the concept of the backhand or strokes, which one could play over the head when the bird chirped on the non-dominant side. In such moments, she would canter to the rear with her back to her opponent, turn around, face the shuttle and hit it with her forehand. A jest is what she calls this silliness. But these hints foretold her athleticism that she would soon start developing into magic at her whim.

It is challenging to outrun the shuttle and receive it in the same direction. But she was agile, swift, and deliberate in learning by watching her seniors. Once, during a practice session, Padukone called her to join him in a game. She used to be shy back then, and he deliberately tricked the young girl with flicks on the net. The lessons learnt that day went a long way in teaching her the game's complexities.

In Siliguri, to find a regular place to play, her father went out of his way again to repair a broken cement floor and turn it into a serviceable badminton court. It was a stage set-up belonging to a theatre near the Kanchenjunga stadium. He built it into a 14-foot-high structure with walls brushing the baselines. One could smash their racquet into the wall if they weren't careful. It was an unplanned stroke of brilliance as the restrictive dimensions of the court further fuelled the desire in Madhumita to be quick and forceful. The shuttle wouldn't soar high in the air, and one couldn't hover close to the baseline as racquets were few and expensive, so the only way left was to have zippy movements. She practised here extensively and never bothered if anyone else showed up or not.

There were ways through which she could hone her skills by herself. Shadow practice and running at the Kanchenjunga stadium – earlier named Tilak Maidan stadium – would fill her time when there was no one on the other side of the court. Her parents would carry a cane on the rough paths while enjoying the freshness of their routine walk. They also owned a house in Jalpaiguri, a city identified as Siliguri's twin sister. There were badminton players here, so she spent her weekends here, where there was hardly a day's rest. Practice was never an issue; well-wishers were keen to help and practise with her. A doctor from north Bengal, K. C. Mitra, who ran a nursing home, would finish his work in the evening but not his day. He would return home and take Madhumita to an outdoor place for training.

Her father sacrificed a lot to realise his dream, which his daughter accepted as hers. Back in the day, he used to play badminton as well, mostly doubles. He saw to it that the opportunities he didn't receive in his time were available to his eager daughter. Holding a senior position in the office, her father could spare some time to move mountains for her. And he didn't have to travel out of his station. His reputation was unblemished. They would spend about a month in Calcutta, where Madhumita would sharpen her skills, and he would manage his work from there. Once, he couldn't make himself available because of work, so he left Madhumita in the care of his secretary. The secretary's wife and daughter started taking Madhumita to the stadium for practice.

Ministers visited their home in Siliguri and heard tales of Madhumita's deftness in badminton, but they had something more to look forward to during those meets. Her father would honour their visits with a short trip to Darjeeling. Eminent politicians like Subrata Mukherjee and Buddhadeb Bhattacharjee have shared a few knocks with Madhumita.

Good luck and hard work eventually came together when Madhumita joined the Indian senior squad in 1978. Earlier, she had represented the railways in the nationals. Still, her father wanted Madhumita to carry the same pride of belonging to the state of Bengal that every other Bengali in the nation feels for their state. It was only after playing for the Indian team that Madhumita finally accepted the invitation. She played her first international tournament in March of 1978. The ABC tournament, held in China, was her first voyage in international badminton.

Before leaving for her first international tournament, Dipu Ghosh had introduced her to the management at the railways team. Since she was young, a few people raised their eyebrows. In all seriousness, someone suggested changing her age to eighteen so her membership would seem justifiable. But her father chuckled at the request. After returning from China and at the age of, to the curious mind, thirteen years and seven months, she became a part of the Railways badminton roster.

Madhumita has the date of joining carefully framed in one corner of her mind, which is 22 May 1978. Southeastern Railways wasn't willing to let go of her talent, so she was seized. Madhu Dandavate was the Minister of railways back then, revered for his contribution and encouragement of women in sports and public office. She and her family moved to Calcutta to welcome the new undertaking in her life.

Balancing the scales of adolescent life and pursuing her passion was an everyday routine. Her father accompanied her to the practice sessions held at the YMCA (Young Men's Christian Association) in the morning, as she was too young to travel alone. She would have to return home to change into the sari that was her school uniform. Once school finished for the day, it would be time for the sun to tuck into the horizon. But the day would still not be over for Madhumita. She would again leave to churn out a few more hours of practice. This schedule had become too tiring for young Madhumita. To ease the pressure, her father decided to relocate. They moved to the southwest of Calcutta, a suburb named Behala.

Near their home was Eastern Railway's officer's colony, which had a cemented badminton court. She recalls two young boys who were almost of similar age. They tried to match her growing pace, limited by nothing but her will. Soon, she convinced her father to let her travel alone. She took the bus or even the tram, which was the artery of Calcutta. Her father made sure she knew how to soar and was prepared when the tides come in the life of a blossoming sportsperson. She was growing up.

When Madumita came to Calcutta for state tournaments, her father would give her soothing massages using mustard oil, make breakfast, and tie her shoelaces. He wanted her to only concentrate on her warm-up and practice sessions. Once, she had to attend trials at the Southeastern Railway Garden, and she was donning a skirt. Her father had acute skill in raising a star but limited wisdom in hooking a skirt. He fastened the metal pins incorrectly. On realising the slip-up, he rushed in search of a household in the neighbourhood that could possess the invaluable, albeit momentarily, needle and thread. This handy tool pair was and still is expected in most Indian houses. From time to time, it has lent its service to the ladies who, with a mix of training and some art, would fix the attires that adorn their loved ones. One such lady offered help, and Madhumita had a skirt to wear. It was an instance that imparted lifelong skills. Her father displayed how strong willpower could be and how it can supersede circumstances.

Her first senior nationals title in singles came in 1981. She dethroned Ami who had six singles tiles until then at the forty-sixth national open championships. A steady Madhumita defeated her opponent 4–11, 4–11. Ami, despite her superior stroke-play, showed quite an inferior control of the game and lacked better judgement. Madhumita possessed both agility and powerful smashes. Those tools paved her way to the final, not allowing Ami to recover during multiple occasions in the final. If only Madhumita could improve her anticipation at this point, then it could take her a long way in both the domestic as well as the international circuit.

India saw the speed and raw power with which she moved on the court. Her second singles title final against Ami in 1984 saw some quick movements and captivating strokes. And yet again in 1985, against Ami in the final, she could be seen everywhere on the court, traversing with ease and at the same time pushing the shuttle with power. Ami's singles reign was officially over. Indian female players had weaker backhands. But Madhumita was the only one who could use her speed and reach the shuttle with a round-the-head stroke. Against Ami, she would target this same weakness and persistently attack her backhand from all corners of the court. Eventually, an aging Ami would buckle, awarding Madhumita with points, confidence and glory. From 1984 to 1990, Madhumita won seven consecutive singles titles in the nationals.

She was a formidable doubles player, too, proven by her eight titles in women's doubles and twelve in mixed doubles. Some of her notable partners were Ami, P. V. V. Lakshmi, Sanat Misra, Harjeet Singh, and Vinod Kumar. Internationally, she won a bronze medal in the women's team event at the 1982 Asian Games held in New Delhi and another bronze in the women's team event at the 1998 Commonwealth Games held in Kuala Lumpur. She also represented India at the Barcelona Olympics in 1992.

Suresh Goel, whom Madhumita credits as a huge inspiration, had even convinced her father to send her to

Banares to attend a summer camp. She loved watching him play. She emphasised she never saw him catching the shuttle low. His courtcraft was too smooth, combined with stellar anticipation. Madhumita always appreciated Padukone's determination and dedication. During the late 1970s, she started watching Ami play in tournaments. Ami's playing style enamoured Madhumita. She faced her during an All-India tournament in 1978 in Bangalore. Before the match, she only watched her practice and her warm-up routine. Her presence influenced her so much that Madhumita didn't believe she could ever stand against Ami. But it was only a matter of time before she would go on to defeat her idol. Dipu Ghosh had remarked once how Madhumita had gained a lot from playing with Ami and how it proved to be of benefit to her.

Madhumita realised that badminton is also about mental fortitude. She was known for screaming and shrieking on the court. Those weren't signs of exasperation but tactical moves. She believed in shouting a few decibels higher to unnerve her opponent, if they tried the same strategy. She once gave the same advice to Sindhu. But she confesses how it also helped encourage herself and provided confidence in times of need on the court.

As someone who has always loved being with people and cherished every minute she spent with them, she wonders how times have changed as well as the priorities of the youth. Today, she likes coaching young boys and girls and helping them discover their potential while enjoying the process. The importance she gave to discipline during her career is an aspect she tries to inculcate in her students using the right amount of strictness.

On not receiving the Padma Shri honours, Madhumita curiously enquired, 'Do you think that I deserve the Padma Shri?', displaying the modesty she was known for. Soon, realising that she had enough accolades in her name to qualify for the prestigious award, she confessed she didn't check the procedure for applying. Her father started enquiring about the necessary steps, and soon, the West Bengal government asked for her biodata and certificates. A feature titled 'Well done Didi', written by Rakesh Rao in the *Sportstar* magazine, was the best farewell tribute following her retirement, and qualified as an equivalent of certificates that one preserves and flips through as a memoir of nostalgic moments. She shared the same with the government officials! Madhumita didn't receive the award that year. In any case, she missed the deadline. She re-applied in the subsequent year and eventually received it in 2006.

Madhumita recalls how players in her time were not worried about what they said or what information they divulged to journalists. They held their racquet high and mighty and kept their business limited to the game. There was still time for politics and diplomacy to enter the frame of badminton. Unfortunately, there isn't a picture yet that captures Ami, Madhumita and Aparna, the grand achievers in Indian badminton, together. Three ruling queens from different eras are yet to be seen in the same snapshot.

She is fond of Ami for the care and affection tightly encased in Ami's generosity for Madhumita. Ami pampered her. Treated as a younger sister irrespective of their gruelling battles on the court, Madhumita feels proud she comes from a time when it was possible to earn the concern and goodwill of one's sturdiest rivals.

16

Pullela Gopi Chand: Architect of Indian Badminton Renaissance

PULLELA GOPI CHAND DREAMED of taking badminton to every nook and corner of the country. It was tough, but Gopi was equally determined. He wanted to make a mark by embracing glory as a player and then as a coach. He confronted obstacles on and off the court and, every time, emerged wiser. His single-minded devotion to badminton inspired hundreds of youngsters to choose the game as a career option. Gopi was the reason.

Gopi is a significant chapter in Indian badminton. Student. Teacher. Learning and then giving it back to the game through coaching. His unstinted contribution has created a playfield where youngsters can look forward to making a place for themselves under the guidance of one of India's finest athletes. Gopi has been a great success story.

It was Padukone who triggered his love for badminton. Drawing inspiration from the legend, Gopi emulated his idol's feat of winning the All-England title in 2001. Not many backed him to return with the biggest win of his career.

Gopi defeated Singapore's Ronald Susilo 15–11, 15–12 in forty-five minutes in the first match. Next, he eliminated local challenger Colin Haughton 15–7, 15–4. It took him a mere half hour to dismiss Haughton. It was to get tough as Gopi was to meet China's Ji Xinpeng, the Olympic champion, in the pre-quarterfinal. Gopi won 15–3, 15–9.

Gopi was on song. Anders Boesen from Denmark was the challenger in the quarterfinal. In Gopi's favour, the verdict was 15–11, 15–7.

Gopi had surpassed his expectations. Playing in the semifinal was a dream come true. Peter Gade, the top seed from Denmark, stood in his path. Gopi conceded seven points from leading 13–6, and a 13–13 score was worrying indeed. It became 14–14 before Gopi won the following three points. The contest left the audience in a trance, with the score tied at 14–14 after Gopi had led 13–8. Gopi made it 16–15 and finally 17–15 as he stormed into the final. Only Padukone and Nath had travelled that distance in the past.

For Gopi, it tested his resilience against Chen Hong of China. Tactically, Gopi decided to exploit the opponent's fitness since he had played a tiring semifinal against Malaysian star Roslin Hashim. Trailing 10–12, Gopi reeled off five points in a row to take the first game. Gopi then tightened his grip, led 10–5 in the second game and closed the contest at 15–6. The genial Hyderabadi, at twenty-eight, had made the nation proud, considerably boosting badminton in India.

From a game played open-air in parks, badminton developed into an attractive indoor competition on the strength of some compelling courtcraft exponents. It managed to catch the attention of sports lovers at every stage of society – from schools to colleges. In later years, the game secured a following large enough for institutions to offer financial security by providing jobs to players.

Gopi had the intent to go far. Like most youngsters in India, he also liked cricket, but his innate skills in badminton ensured he kept his focus on conquering the court. 'I knew my court was my domain, and nothing excited me more than that I could dominate my court. I could retrieve the shuttle from any corner, any angle.'

It was not just putting the shuttle across the net. Landing it into the corners with some deft placements was an art. And Gopi had developed his game into an exhibition of skills, whether a cross-court smash or a delightful drop.

For Gopi to look at badminton as a career was a glorious peep into the future. In a city which took pride in its association with cricket, hockey and football, it was a step into a new field – badminton. There were few encouraging facilities, but Gopi was fortunate to come across Arif, a dedicated coach. Arif's devotion paved the way for Hyderabad to adopt badminton as the primary sport even as more youngsters looked at professional attachment to the game.

Padukone was the reason many took up badminton, and Gopi was no different. 'Thanks to Prakash sir; if it had not been for his win, we probably would never have imagined that Indians could win something like an All-England. Prakash sir's win was huge, impacting everybody, especially our generation. Maybe this generation probably doesn't remember it as much. And his win, at least, could make us believe in the dream that an Indian can win the All-England,' Gopi reflected on his love for badminton.

It could have been smoother sailing. The need for proper facilities was a significant hindrance. Lack of competition also meant that Gopi had to work that much harder. 'In my growing days, what had happened was the levels had dropped from where Prakash sir had left. It went down from the 1980s, where he dominated and played well. He won at a time when we struggled to reach the last sixteen of any significant event. The 1990s were horrible, and everything in 1983, 1984, and 1985 was still better. Modi was still at the Commonwealth level, but we weren't at the Asian Games or the world level. Until 2001, when I won, there were no wins. We would go to tournaments only to lose in the first or second rounds.'

Gopi is candid. 'To win, even if I look at it dispassionately, was big. I think it was almost like going from negative to a realistic position. When I won, at least the people in Hyderabad with whom I interacted started to think that if Gopi Anna could win, we too could. When I talked to a Kashyap or a Saina, they said we could also win playing here. And then I started the same way: if I could win, they could. Prakash sir had this legacy that he trained in Indonesia. He went to Denmark, stayed in Denmark, and then won. Those options were not there. I was here in Hyderabad, and I was there in Bangalore, and I won from our system. So that made people more confident, and that helped us win.'

The question that confronted badminton lovers was why India did not produce another All-England champion after Gopi. 'It was by chance, in a way. It so happens that you win many tournaments but not the tournaments you should have. So that's one thing. Why didn't Saina win? Why didn't Sindhu win? It beats purpose because every Super Series played almost has the same level. It's like an Indonesian Open which Saina has won three times. It is on the same level as the Olympics. But what happens is the conditions at All-England need you to be physically much stronger. And I think our players have lost out in a way, and we haven't done that well in slow, hard conditions. But I'm sure we will get there soon.'

His humility comes to the fore. 'For me, I was very fortunate that I had people who coached me at different times. But they were God-sent. I had Hamid Hussein sir, who made me love the sport. Arif sir taught me discipline in the sport. Prakash sir taught me how to stay focused and calm and achieve purpose. Ganguly Prasad taught me how to be friendly and be part of the journey at a higher level. I was also fortunate to have a couple of foreign coaches who left things in my mind about how they trained me, which I remember every day of my training. I've been very fortunate that my build-up, whether it's my injury or whether it's my general training, has almost made me the coach I am, because all of them have had a great impact on my coaching style and coaching ways.'

For all his love for the game, Gopi had to make the hard decision to call it quits even when his heart wanted him to continue. 'I think with all of us, injuries have been a definite reason. The last few years of my career, I knew I had only so much because I had had three left knee surgeries, one right knee surgery and two broken metatarsals.

'The last few years, I could have pushed, but every moment I played, it reminded me that I was playing at the expense of another athlete who could be playing better. Or if I coach, will it be more productive than playing, and if playing at a subpar level was unacceptable to me. I wanted to avoid going to a World Championship or the All-England. Go there with the idea that I could not beat these three players. If a semifinal was to be my best result, it was unacceptable to me. If I didn't think I had a chance to win, then I would rather not play. I hastened to leave the sport because I could see a Saina, a Kashyap, and a Sindhu; all were waiting for me to coach. I said I should coach because I thought I was being too selfish by continuing to play.'

The game's commercialisation meant that badminton players could now claim to be celebrities in a society that did not look beyond cricketers as role models in sports. Badminton players became big stars, seen in hoardings and endorsing products. Badminton players can now avail themselves of the facilities previously limited to cricketers.

How did Gopi look at these developments? 'I think it's something which is, in a way, good, a positive direction to move in because not many people see this as inspiration. Some of us who played the sport for the love of sport forget what we earned from the sport. There's a generation today that asks what they will get if they win. For that, I think it's important that you have these motivations, which are very, very good. And I feel thrilled to see the rise of the sport, to see the rise of the stars in the sport because only with the rise of the stars, I think the rise of the sport will happen.'

Coming to Hyderabad from Ongole at the age of eleven was the trigger point for Gopi. The Lal Bahadur Shastri Stadium was close to where he stayed, and he chose badminton because it was the most affordable sport for Gopi. It was decided that he would concentrate on badminton, and the responsibility was on his mother, Subbaravamma, to ensure he did not lose interest in the game. It helped Gopi that Hussein was a caring coach to learn the game from in the initial stages. Thanks to Hussein's guidance, Gopi progressed rapidly.

Sanjay Sharma praised Gopi, 'He was a hard-working player. He started the jump smash, and I have always admired him for his reading of the game. I am so happy to see him develop into a coach and produce world champions at his academy in Hyderabad.'

Gopi's habit of waking up early enabled him to effectively plan his day – school, training, studies and rest. He had Hussein train him early in his career, and then Arif came as an angel to transform his approach to badminton. Arif gave Gopi the comfort of sustained coaching and new shuttles in abundance. 'Getting new shuttles was a boon,' remembers Gopi. Expectedly, Gopi had the right decision to pursue, and who was better than Hussein and Arif to shape his destiny?

He has followed a philosophical path, taking the failures in his stride. 'The way I would put it is that I've had my ups and downs. I was very fortunate to have family support, whether it was my mother, father or wife; whenever I was down, they took guard and protected me and then didn't let this whole programme go adrift. I think it's not about me alone; this journey is about us. They took the brunt of it whenever I was down and shielded me.'

He reiterates the support of his family. 'It's God's grace that I have parents who kept supporting me.' He was not present to witness the birth of his children and saw them only in brief phases during their growing years. He had no time for any of the family events and hardly attended any weddings in the family. 'They never gave me any family responsibilities. Yeah. I took my wife out for the first holiday ten years after we got married.' It's almost like Gopi was wedded to this sport.

How does he manage to keep the family happy now with such a heavy workload? 'Nine o'clock, I must sleep. I have to start my session at 4:15 a.m. I told my family and friends I can't come for any of these things.'

The inspiration in the early stages of his career came from the mentions in the newspapers and magazines. 'It is a perception thing for me. There was a time when we were put on the cover or the centre spread of *Sportstar* magazine. That was the ultimate. That was enough. Today, in terms of quantity, the media may be huge, and exposure might be huge. Back then, the quality of the pictures and writing was much more in many ways. That's my perception. Being featured in newspapers and *Sportstar* was a huge motivation. For us, *Sportstar* was the national newspaper for sports. The Arjuna Award and Khel Ratna were indeed huge.'

Gopi Chand has a supporter in Manjusha to discuss the game. 'After 1994, I was with Gopi Chand. We used to discuss a lot of badminton. He would come for my matches. He wanted me to be in his academy and train. I learnt a lot from Gopi. He had some limitations, but he worked very hard. He would return from tours and ask me to do certain things he would have observed. He was teaching what the coaches could not, like dragging the legs. He played best from 1999 to 2001, and those were the three great years when he found power and confidence in his attack and developed a perfect net game. He has been successful as a player and a coach, too,' said Manjusha.

As Gopi observed, awards meant a lot. 'Awards are earned. Today, when you go to athletes, they look at the financial gains, one crore, two crores. Their priorities are different from ours. It matters to them what you gain from awards. Today, if you approach them for a shoot for a centre spread, they may ask you for money. Can you blame them? They have to secure their future financially. For us, it did not matter what you got from the award. Things and times have changed, and it is unfair to compare.'

Icons will be forever, and Gopi speaks his mind. 'Prakash (Padukone) sir, (Sunil) Gavaskar sir will always be remembered. Today, if you ask me who is on the cricket team, I will know only a few players. Players like Dhanraj (Pillay) and Mukesh (Kumar) are known even today. We know them for their accomplishments. We have yet to learn about today's national champions. It is sad if I ask five people on the road who won the silver at the London Olympics, they won't even know. So, this quantitative media space does not contribute to remembering our icons and achievers. A few years later, I won't be surprised if you forget these modern athletes.'

Gopi and V. V. S Laxman are strikingly similar in their presence on the sporting field. They are not aggressive and certainly not at all demonstrative. What could be the reason? 'Perception of the media and sponsors want people to turn that way, which is very sad. Their personalities differ, but the sponsors want them to be loud and brash. And the media managers are also telling them that this is what sells. That is unfortunate. They are faking their personality for fame, money and stuff. They think this is the new cool. Unfortunately, it shows a lack of grooming.'

His thoughts on discipline are clear, and he does not leave room for compromise. 'From a discipline perspective, I may not be shouting and screaming, but at least the discipline is maintained. And that's also an important aspect of the academy's culture, which I'm pleased about. Discipline is key, and you've been able to manage it. So, if I'm strict or not, I think that's a question probably answered better by the students.'

Two aspects of his character stood out in his hour of glory. Thanks to Dr Ashok Rajgopal, he conquered a career-threatening knee injury suffered in 1994. Gopi remembered Dr Rajgopal with gratitude the day he won the All-England. On achieving stardom, he turned down a lucrative soft drink endorsement. 'I don't want youngsters to do what I won't,' was Gopi's explanation.

One of the most significant decisions that changed badminton in India was when Gopi decided to give back to the sport once he quietly faded away from the competitive circuit. 'Gopi's move to take up coaching was perhaps one of the turning points which had a sweeping impact on the entire badminton fraternity itself,' insisted Subrahmanyam. For someone who played across the world at the highest level in the most demanding conditions – especially given the kind of indifferent patronage the sport got at home and abroad – Gopi was quick to realise the importance of guiding the destiny of players who had the potential to make it big.

'It was not just about teaching the sport's finer aspects but more about preparing the players mentally and physically for the huge challenges they face as they move to dream big and try to chase the goals successfully,' Subrahmanyam said. Gopi – who Arif groomed at Fateh Maidan, where even shuttles were at a premium to train – was conscious that the essence of quality coaching lay in first ensuring the proper facilities and atmosphere for the players to train.

The champion shuttler was equally aware that more than just coaching or long hours of conditioning programmes, it was about getting the players the desired kind of exposure. Subrahmanyam added, 'Perhaps this is one area where Gopi stands apart from the rest of his contemporaries in modern-day sport when it comes to coaching. 'My first target is to see that the players get what I missed when I was playing,' has been his motto. And his emphasis on scientific training rather than going through the daily routines of putting the shuttle back in play was another significant shift in the coaching he initiated.'

Gopi ensured he had his way while taking care of the players' interests in all aspects, steering clear of any controversial moves that would ruffle the feathers of the big bosses of Indian badminton. Not surprisingly, Gopi soon assumed multiple roles, from a coach to an administrator to holding an office-bearer's post, for he knew what kind of hurdles one faced at different stages and levels in making a big player. Once he got the clearance from the Badminton Association of India to mentor the cream of Indian badminton, Gopi charted out his own plan of action, ensuring there was little interference in executing it to near perfection.

'The setting up of Gopi Chand Academy, thanks to the generosity of Nimmagadda Prasad, who donated about ₹ 3 crores to start the work in 2008, was another milestone in Indian badminton from where the players only looked one way – upwards and moved in the right direction,' Subrahmanyam emphasised. There was no doubt that Gopi had the hunger to produce champions and had players like Saina who could go the distance in realising his goals and helping her mentor and guru achieve his objective, too.

'I always dreamt of producing an Olympic medallist when I started this Academy,' Gopi once said, and that wish was fulfilled in the 2012 London Olympics when Saina won a bronze. In fact, that magnificent feat of Saina, who by then had already won innumerable Super Series titles, triggered a revolution in Indian badminton, especially with more girls taking up the sport.

To Gopi's delight, shuttlers like Saina, Kidambi Srikanth, B. Sai Praneeth, H. S. Prannoy, and Sindhu have only reminded the world that he has left an indelible mark as a coach. 'Yes, there were instances when questions were raised about the sport, but the success stories that have swept them under the carpet were also a tribute to his management skills even while ensuring that there was no drift in his original scheme of things – to keep producing champions,' Subrahmanyam pointed out.

Sports Authority of India's ample support helped set up another SAI-Gopi Chand Academy, now the hub of national camps for Indian shuttlers preparing for major tournaments. 'Yes, the jarring note of how Sindhu left him to be on her own just after being crowned World Champion was a patch that the badminton fraternity would have loved to avoid. By all means, Gopi, as a coach, has contributed significantly to Indian badminton,' concluded Subrahmanyam.

17

Aparna Popat: The Queen of the Court

Whether it was playing catch up and cricket, arranging a table and turning it into her first experiment with table tennis, or loving the arduous sport of tennis, there's no sport that Aparna Popat hasn't tried. Steffi Graf was her first idol. When she was eight and a half, during her summer vacations, her mother got tired of this menace in the house. She took her to a club. Naturally, Aparna wanted to see the tennis courts first. But destiny had already started conspiring. To enrol in tennis, she would have to wait. Her mother took her to the badminton courts next.

They procured the required information and the form, and when they were about to leave, her mother's friend, who was also around, asked them to meet the coach on the last court. He only offered personal coaching but agreed to induct Aparna. He called her to a different club the next day, Sachivalaya Gymkhana in Mumbai. On seeing Aparna, he made her do a few basic exercises, nothing more than running and jumping jacks. Not even five minutes had passed, and he asked her mother to start sending her to the club for badminton lessons. Aparna hadn't held a badminton racquet until then.

That was where they had the life-changing encounter with the coach, Anil Pradhan, who refused any payment from Aparna's parents but tutored her in badminton. Equipped with white canvas Bata shoes and a simple racquet, Aparna started a meaningful journey. He taught her footwork, educated her on concepts and then didn't allow her to step onto the courts for the first month!

Aparna fast-forwarded her journey from wall practice to winning her first nationals (under-12) using her avidness for the sport and resilience to practise seven days a week. It didn't matter if it was her birthday or her 10th board exams. She was on the court every day. The only holiday was the final day of Ganesh Chaturthi festival. Being a Maharashtrian, that was one day Pradhan was ready to make an exception.

'Aparna's success was insured when Anil's eye caught her talent. During her formative stages, she did not know how to even hold the racquet. She was raw when Anil took her under his wings. He taught her all the deceptive strokes that he himself used to employ during his prime. They worked tirelessly for 365 days of the year. There were no holidays for them, Anil had drilled this expectation into her from early on. Her talent and desire to aim for the sky found the right teacher,' says Nadkarni.

Aparna's love for tennis was still simmering. She used to carry an extra tennis racquet in her bag for some wall practice before her badminton classes commenced at 3 p.m. every day. It helped her warmup. She would look for every opportunity to find herself in and around the tennis courts. She would serve as a ball girl during matches or even when her cousin, who trained in the same club, used to play. The tennis coaches never complained about the extra helping hand, and Aparna enjoyed being close to tennis.

After her first victory in the nationals, one of the tennis coaches who had his eye on Aparna's tryst with tennis called her mother and suggested that she take tennis lessons. He was confident she could be a national champion in tennis as well. But her mother felt she was already performing well at badminton and was on the road to great success.

It does appeal to Aparna occasionally to think how familiarity with several sports might have shaped her game imperceptibly. Fast-paced table tennis practice against the wall and catch practice in cricket must have honed her reflexes. Those extra runs to cricket coaching camps were valuable. Some transfer of skills is unmistakably noticeable. The slice that one could play at the net was borrowed from tennis, and her defensive stance looked similar to that in table tennis. She was greatly inspired by Graf. Wimbledon used to be a fortnight that she would look forward to.

The life of Nadia Comaneci, the Romanian gymnast who was a five-time Olympic gold medallist, also inspired the young Aparna after she watched a film about Nadia's struggles and determination to succeed. Another memory forever etched in Aparna's mind was of a tournament in Pune where Padukone was the chief guest. After the game ended, Padukone signed autographs for fans. When it was Aparna's turn, he first signed a card for her and then looked up and said, 'Well played.' That someone of Padukone's stature noted and praised her play was thrilling for the young badminton hopeful.

Aparna didn't give her parents a chance to object to her playing. She was performing equally well in academics. She understood her parents were encouraging because they realised soon enough what made her happy. And as a parent herself today, she realises it's satisfying for one to know that. Pradhan, her coach, made a bold statement when he announced that he would prove her to be the P. T. Usha of badminton, even before she won her first nationals. But for Aparna and her parents, it was more about doing what puts a smile on her face.

Her school gave enough importance to Aparna, unparalleled by anything she had received before. But she was also shy.

After winning a tournament, the school principal summoned her, and she had to carry her trophy from her classroom to the office. To add to her jitters, the principal was not a big sports fan. Upon reaching the office, Aparna received a stern congratulatory message, highlighted with the warning that she could not let her grades drop. She loved playing in front of people and their engrossed gaze during a game, but she did not feel the same way when collecting a trophy.

She had her share of struggles while at school. Once, she was sick and the junior nationals were a week away. Her coach advised her to get permission to skip school as otherwise, it would become too strenuous. Her mother had to face the principal. The principal reluctantly sanctioned the leave, not before letting her mother know what she felt about sports as a career. She also warned her it would be the last time such permission would be granted. At times, when Bombay Gymkhana hosted tournaments, she had to shuttle between playing matches and going back to school to attend class tests.

Between the age of eleven and fourteen, when a child is exploring the expanse of her strengths, a lot of equipment is required to support such an endeavour. And that requires financial investment. Frequently buying boxes of shuttles, shoes and racquets meant Aparna's parents had to cut back on many other things. Her mother accompanied Aparna during tournaments, and all of this was additional expenditure. Aparna's older sister never complained about the focus Aparna was receiving.

Aparna felt lucky when she got a scholarship from Puma at the age of twelve. It entailed six T-shirts, six shorts and two pairs of shoes. Even though it was all basic, it indeed helped her family. The strain eased when she was awarded another scholarship when she was fourteen. Air India – which invested substantially in sports then – had bequeathed the scholarship and took care of shuttles and other equipment that is part of a badminton kit. Looking back, Aparna recalled how those sponsorships were timely and paved a smoother path for her journey.

She next won a runners-up medal in the under-15 category before winning the singles in that age group for the next two years. In the last year of playing under-15, she also finished runner-up in the under-18s. It was a steady progression for her up the competitive ladder. After appearing for her 10th board exams at the age of sixteen, she moved to Bangalore to train at Padukone's academy a few months before its official inauguration. There, the distinction between sports academies and coaching centres became strikingly clear to Aparna.

'An academy is one where people are way more serious and organised and work to produce champions systematically. And it can be at the school or district level as well. There's a focus on fitness, provision of stay and insightful mentoring. And Padukone's academy was the first of its kind,' she reflected. With few people initially, including Padukone and Vimal, Aparna received proper mentoring, which she considered the best she had ever experienced.

She recalled how Padukone's gameplay was devoid of mistakes, preceded by a minimal 1980s warmup style. His half-smashes on the line are unforgettable. To impress him, she had to push herself to her limits. On his enquiry if she had tired herself out or not, she would lie while panting. Manjusha, Dipankar Bhattacharjee and others, all seniors to her, also joined the academy. It gave her immense exposure to focused play. Compare that to her training in Mumbai – where her day started with twenty sit-ups, ten push-ups, a few minutes of skipping and then some kangaroo jumps that would put the agony to an end. She used to run three rounds of the ground during her summer holidays as part of her training for junior nationals.

Soon, her famous run of victories in the nationals began. It was complemented by medal-winning performances at the international level too. Before her first singles title in nationals, she had reached the finals for two years. She was knocking on the doors of senior nationals.

There was an inescapable equation between playing at the international and the national levels. To get an opportunity to represent India abroad, one had to be in the national team. They also had to be national champions to be on the team. To counter the forces conspiring not to see Aparna on the team, she recalled this statement reiterated umpteen times by Pradhan. He would say, 'You have to be number one. Not number two. Number two to eight are all the same. Reasons will be concocted to keep you out.' To be rooted and unmovable, you had to be a national champion. But to start her streak, she also had to breach the iron door that was stopping her. The two losses in the finals of singles at the nationals for the last two years were a cause of concern.

Aparna requested Pradhan to travel to the 1997 nationals to be held at Hyderabad. His motivating words and presence always invoked the indomitable spirit in Aparna. In the semifinals, she faced P. V. V. Lakshmi, for whom it was home turf. During the game, Aparna twisted her ankle but managed to cruise through. The pain refused to subside, and neither did Pradhan.

On the morning of the final, Aparna complained of her agony to him, but he coaxed her into playing. The only medical attention available to her was an icebag. She was playing against Manjusha, who was the defending champion. Lakshmi, who had two singles titles, had recovered after a recent knee surgery. She participated in the tournament against her doctor's advice and refused to go down quickly against Aparna.

Lakshmi lacked deep tosses, and Aparna was smart enough to consistently take advantage of the weakness. The final proved to be a walk in the park for Aparna. She defeated the four-time champion, Manjusha, 11–1 and 11–4. The match lasted about twenty-one minutes, half the time it took Gopi Chand to defend his singles title. The first game saw Aparna using powerful forehand smashes from her toolkit to break Manjusha's solid demeanour – and it worked. Manjusha aimed for deep tosses but lacked precision and steadiness, costing her crucial points with the shuttle extending beyond the boundaries of the court.

Manjusha regained her poise in the second game to slow down its pace. The service had changed sixteen times before the score was 3–3. Aparna returned the game's pace to her own with a barrage of cross-court and mid-court smashes, catching Manjusha off-guard. Aparna's speed and easy court coverage ensured her first singles crown.

Her second consecutive singles title of 1998 saw her defeating Neelima Choudary in the semifinal with some quaint drops and effortless dribbles. At the same time, Lakshmi defeated Manjusha, since all four semifinals took place simultaneously, against the custom. In the final against Lakshmi, Aparna set up an easy victory for herself, with the score being 11–3 and 11–4. Aparna combined some well-placed drop-shots with unforced errors made on Lakshmi's part to reach the finish line faster.

A young Aparna observed that quarters and semis were always more challenging, shining light on the criticism, made by many, about the game's competitiveness. Nevertheless, Aparna shared the victory podium once again with Gopi Chand, and was on her way to winning seven more single titles.

Even though she was training at Padukone's Academy, Pradhan predicted the match's score much before she was to clinch that victory. From here onwards, she would win nine consecutive singles titles in the nationals. It is a feat achieved only by Padukone in the history of Indian badminton.

After that, every year, one month before the nationals, Aparna would devote all her focus to preparation. Each national and the victories that came along were different and unique for her. Looking back, she sometimes found it hard to believe how she maintained a consistent form, to be seen as a force to be reckoned with for eleven consecutive years.

By the last nationals in 2005, Aparna developed a pain in her wrist. The pain was severe to the extent that she was able to practise only once a week. Her physiotherapist declared her to be crazy since, on suggesting not even to attempt playing the tournament, she received a stoic negative response from Aparna. She had nothing to lose. Having an illustrious career both at the national and the international level, Aparna could afford such a risk with some ingenuity. Or at least what it seemed like to the people watching her. She started the tournament with an exclusive backhand service because a forehand would send a shooting pain in her wrist.

Everyone thought she had developed a new strategy. As the tournament progressed, it grew even tougher. She could not tap or push on the backhand, as it required the wrist to be involved. Her goal now was to survive and not exit due to an injury. It might have even seemed like the world was against her, as the semifinal was a long, arduous match spilling into the third game. But she still managed to surpass her opponent.

Then came the final against Saina, who confidently stated that she was about to win her first title in the senior nationals, proving all the emphatic expectations to be justified. But Aparna was about to defy all odds.

Battling her inner voice, the possibility of it being her last nationals and the agonising wrist pain, Aparna proved her mettle to a stunned audience. She proudly recalls, 'It was just the best finale one could hope for. Getting a standing ovation from the residents of Bangalore, mentored by Mr Padukone and setting a record, all of these are an unforgettable memory.'

There was something about that day as things fell into place for her, like a puzzle that finds its last missing piece. But what still amazes Aparna as she tries to demystify a riddle is how the wrist pain made its unwelcome return the following day. She believes it was fate. But her humility speaks for itself when the people around her learn of her determination and hard work.

The badminton world unequivocally admires Aparna when assessing the performance of Indian players internationally. Her stride began with a silver medal in the singles of the World Junior Championship. Two years later, the Commonwealth Games took place in Kuala Lumpur, Malaysia, in 1998. Aparna was in her prime and in excellent form. She secured a silver in the individual singles. But she distinctly remembers the team championships because of the positive atmosphere. Both men's and women's teams cheered for each other. And they brought home a bronze medal. It was her first multi-sports competition.

The same year, the Asian Games took place, but as Aparna remarked, Indians weren't meeting the required standards. Asian Games have always enjoyed a higher stature in terms of quality because of the countries participating and their expertise in respective sports. 'We were complacent that we had qualified for the tournament.'

In 2000, Aparna headed to the Sydney Olympic Games as India's only women's badminton representative. Any player qualifying for the Olympics would be on cloud nine. And she learnt it's not only the training for matches that matters but also the off-court preparation. It includes proper mentoring and instilling the belief that one can do it.

There are ample protocols during a multi-sport event, and it can get overwhelming for a player attending for the first time. Questions like where does one have to report on entering the games village? How to receive one's personal luggage which arrives later? Where's the mess? Is there a physiotherapist? From where can they take the bus? Can they ask for extra practice? Where to get the shuttles for practice? Can they pack their food and carry it to the stadium? And many more only morph the tournament into a giant monster in the player's imagination.

She explained how the government would sanction eight tournaments in a year, and those used to be the prime picks of that era. They were the All-England, French, Dutch, Danish, and German Open in the European circuit and Singapore, Malaysian, and Indonesian Open in Asia. Due to seedings, they would run into the top players in the first or second rounds. 'Getting fewer matches to play, a lack of feedback structure and planning on returning home would result in an average experience,' said Aparna.

In 2002, Aparna won a bronze medal in singles at the Commonwealth Games held in Manchester, England, after losing to Tracey Hallam of England. In an irritated tone, she remembered how her coaches heavily criticised her for losing to her opponent. Aparna felt terrible at the time for being castigated even after clinching a medal, but later, she saw it as a proud moment of her life. As mentioned, her wrist pain was unbearable by 2005, and she played at two-thirds of her potential. She even endured emotional blackmailing by Indian officials.

'I was forced to play during the Uber Cup held in Jaipur. I told them I had pain, but they retorted by saying how could I refuse to play for the country. It made my pain even worse,' said an anguished Aparna. She participated in a few more tournaments, but the pain always returned. She consulted multiple specialists, but nothing helped.

Aparna felt she got everything, and what she didn't, she dug out. The primary issue was her self-belief that she was not good enough. Adding to it was a rough transition from juniors to seniors. After reaching the finals of the World Junior Championship, an official congratulated her on her return for paving the way for the junior team, which meant a more straightforward clearance for future participation. Nadkarni remembers some of her words in detail, 'When you hit a smash, either you hit it into the body or just two inches away from their racquet on either side. One doesn't need to go for an exaggerated shot to score a point. Even if the opponent manages to return it, you will most likely get a *halwa* (an easy shot) in the middle of the court which you can easily convert into a point.' Her observation, study of the game and the ability to execute, all rewarded her with nine consecutive singles titles in nationals including a victory against a rising star like Saina.

For Aparna, it was a dilemma. With no particular focus on her future specifically, things looked dreary to her. She had played and matched players in the tournament who went on to be the best in the world.

'It was a pattern where if you could rival the top players of World Junior Championships, then it showed potential to do well at the senior level too,' said Aparna. But she needed guidance. In 2006, when she was about to retire, a famous Indonesian player saw her play and told her how he was impressed by her game. It made her think what could have made the difference. Could playing for a foreign club, better coaching, sports science or conscious planning and scheduling have made the impact she sought?

The precious moments that bejewelled her career are what made it worthwhile for Aparna, more than the titles and the prizes. After winning one of the singles titles at the nationals in Hyderabad, Padukone approached her and said, 'This is how I would have won.' A little later, she ran into Vimal to confirm the statement's veracity. 'Watching you play today reminded me of Prakash.' For her, it was the most valuable compliment she had ever received about how she had played.

She has preserved all her old racquets. She has the ones that she used during the World Junior Championships. However, a particular favourite is one that she had been gifted by Padukone. Yonex had given Padukone a racquet for testing. He played with it for a while and then gave it to Aparna, saying it suited her style. The racquet became an extension of her arm, and later, she got Yonex to build more of the same racquet for her. But she treasures the first one, because it was given to her by Padukone.

Aparna is now immersed in coaching at the National Sports Club of India, using modern techniques to help her better understand her students. She is not demanding and tackles their challenges in a measured way. She makes the trainees play to their strengths – a career in coaching beckons one of India's best women's badminton players.

18

Jwala Gutta: Rebel with a Cause

JWALA GUTTA NEVER BELIEVED in accepting things she disagreed with. Her outspoken attitude might have even harmed her career as she incurred the wrath of the officials. It would not be wrong to say that the authorities had marked her. It was uncommon for players to protest against the federation, as most preferred silence. However, Jwala raised her voice against what she perceived as injustice.

Subrahmanyam revealed, 'Not many are aware of the fact that after the legendary Padukone, who won a bronze in the World Championship, Jwala and Ashwini Ponnappa were the second Indians to win a medal in the World Championship – women's doubles bronze in 2011.'

Subrahmanyam added, 'Quite often, many felt how Jwala could have fared in singles given her reputation to go for the kill at the net with those telling smashes and deceptive drops. But the great Arif sir, her mentor – and who even now trains the young talent at Jwala's academy in Hyderabad – always felt that his champion ward would be better off in doubles, and from the age groups, she won almost every title at stake at the national level in all age groups. The multiple doubles winner in the senior nationals was more adept in half-court coverage, leaving the rest to her partner.'

She was not a rebel in the true sense, but she would not succumb to the administration. She did not promote indiscipline, but Jwala had a penchant for innovation and an unflappable character to stick to her stand. She demonstrated a unique ability to adapt the doubles as the way forward and carried the firepower to bond with her partners and create a space for herself in Indian badminton.

In tennis, John McEnroe and Jimmy Connors come across as fierce individuals who did not hold themselves back from crossing the line. The genius within them allowed them to take the liberty to show a degree of aggression unseen at that level of competition. For Jwala, in later years, it meant a means to voice her anger at being ignored because the federation was keen to promote the achievers in singles.

Jwala quickly realised that she would have to fight for herself in a system that happily presented trophies and mementoes to the singles winners with no prize money involved. In the changing times, she must have been pleased that there was enough money to be made from a career in badminton to live a comfortable life. Jwala decided to play on her own terms. It hurt Jwala when she was mistaken for being rude because of being outspoken. Being outspoken was not common in Indian badminton, but Jwala had a way of making her presence felt. She saw nothing wrong in being an aggressive player.

The fact that she chose to pursue her dreams in doubles meant Jwala was willing to share the honours. In doubles, you learn to play for your partner. If they are weak at the nets, you occupy their place to make the partnership work. In cases where the partner prefers to play up front, you adapt to play at the rear and contribute. It is about backing each other and standing up for each other.

Jwala dominated the net with her ability to anticipate. She was left-handed, which made her a particularly tricky player to compete against. She created angles her opponents found hard to tackle, and Jwala's constant evolution as an expert in doubles made her a dreaded opponent.

Jwala was born to a Telugu father and a Chinese mother. Her father was encouraging regarding his daughter taking up sports. 'I was sure that the sport was going to grow in the country, and I saw talent early in Jwala to ensure she looked for a badminton career,' said Kranti, who would drive sixty kilometres a day on his two-wheeler to provide her training at the Lal Bahadur Shastri Stadium in the heart of Hyderabad. Even though Jwala was good at badminton, swimming, tennis and table tennis, her mother, Yelan, was not keen that she played tennis. For some reason, Yelan thought tennis was for men.

In Hyderabad, Jwala went to noted coach Arif, who taught the best badminton to those in the game's infancy and those who excelled on the big stage. The under-13 title came in 1997, and four years later, she was engaging the attention of those who mattered as she claimed the junior national title.

Jwala was making news when she was hardly ten – always looking to make the headlines with her exploits on the court. She would be motivated by seeing her name in the newspaper. 'I find today the youngsters lack the motivation. Imagine all we looked forward to was a headline in the newspaper and some trophy if you won the title. Today, you win a prize money along with the headlines. That is a huge change from my younger days, and I feel happy for this generation,' she observed.

'Jwala on a dream run…Jwala wins a triple crown… Jwala upsets top seed.' The headlines motivated her. She has fond memories of her rise as a player to watch out for. There was excitement every time she stepped onto the court. Expectations rose with every season, and she worked much harder to maintain the reputation of being a player with a particular style.

She was always concerned about the rights of the players. Jwala would get irritated at the attitude towards women players by an allegedly uncaring officialdom. She often questioned the policy of focusing on the two singles players and treating the doubles pair for only their namesake. 'Once I and my partner (Ashwini Ponnappa) carved a way for doubles, we existed for them. It was always about the singles players being the stars. This discrimination has always been there, and I have spoken against it.'

Jwala had her reasons for being annoyed with the system. She and Ashwini were world number 6 in 2009, but the federation had not given them the due recognition. Jwala's first national title in the doubles came with Shruti Kurien in 2000. An ankle injury interrupted her run, but she and Shruti won it for seven years in succession from 2002, before Jwala partnered with Ashwini in 2009. Jwala and Ashwini won it once more in 2013.

Her magnificent run with Shruti ended when Jwala concluded that their game had reached a point of stagnation. In an interview, Jwala told journalist Shirish Nadkarni that she and Shruti were not going anywhere internationally. 'We were getting stuck at world number 21.' It was a crucial phase in her career, and the move worked as Jwala and Ashwini climbed to the thirteenth spot in the world rankings. In a brilliant move, the pair let go of a few international tournaments and concentrated on the 2010 Commonwealth Games held in New Delhi.

She was equally dominant in the mixed doubles, winning the first title with P. Gopi Chand as her partner in 2003. Two years later, Jwala forged a combination with V. Diju, winning the title five times. She finished with fourteen national titles in doubles and mixed doubles. Jwala, in her way, was a grand achiever and later played the women's and mixed doubles at the 2012 London Olympics.

Ashwini and Jwala made history by winning the doubles gold at the Delhi Commonwealth Games (CWG). It was the first occasion when an Indian pair had won a double gold at the CWG. A packed Siri Fort Stadium cheered Jwala and Ashwini as they tamed the fancied Singaporean pair of Shinta Mulia and Yao Lei in straight games: 21–16, 21–19 on the final day of the games. Jwala and Ashwini were the first women to win gold since Saina Nehwal claimed her title.

The joy of winning the gold was short-lived because of an off-the-court development that Jwala, true to her character, did not attempt to hide. 'One thing I am not happy about was that our federation chief (V. K. Verma) did not even congratulate us after our win. Our president, sitting and watching the match the whole time, did not come to congratulate us,' she was quoted by Press Trust of India.

'When Saina won, he made it a point to congratulate her. Was not our gold also precious to the nation? Of course, you appreciate Saina's gold, but we also won a gold. It was ridiculous of the federation officials. I wanted to change the way our association has worked. I want to change a lot of things in the coming years. This medal will silence my critics. It is my answer to them about whatever happened. I am thrilled, and I would like to say to everyone with negative thoughts about me, just shut up now.'

Jwala states, 'The CWG in Delhi changed the outlook towards women's doubles because we won in front of our home crowds. The media also woke up to the importance of the doubles. The 2010 CWG was the turning point for most games in India. The audience came to discover the quality of our sportspersons.' Jwala regretted that the media highlighted her battles with the BAI more than her on-court feats. 'They (the federation) would not send my entries to international tournaments.' Post-retirement, Jwala became more vocal against the federation officials and advocated different coaches for singles and doubles.

Jwala insisted the federation needed to give more importance to the doubles. 'They get much better equipment and exposure in doubles, but then there is a sense of fear that they should not antagonise the federation officials. In my time, there was loyalty, and there was ethics. When you invest in your partner, it is an emotional bonding. I have played with different partners. I never had any personal issues. We were good on and off the court. I could play with anybody. It has changed now. Players have become a bit selfish. It is different from playing doubles, as in tennis. Off the court, the players now go different ways. They have begun playing politics with the coaches. It is about money and fame. Like the IPL.' Cricketers are seen to be more keen to play the IPL than turn up for their national team.

Known to speak her mind, Jwala may have earned the ire of some of the higher-ups with her comments. She had a decisive view of the role played by the top sportsmen. 'They use social media to promote a product, stay busy thanking the ministers or wishing Sachin Tendulkar a happy birthday. They can do that but also speak on issues. Sadly, they don't think about anybody. I offered my services to get involved with training players in doubles.' She did not hold herself back when it came to protesting against the dress code for women. Many women players were uncomfortable, but not Jwala.

The international federation brought a ruling in 2009 that required women players to wear skirts on the court instead of shorts. Jwala did not mind badminton becoming more glamorous, but she was quoted in the media: 'You cannot make it compulsory for everyone to wear skirts. It depends on each individual and their comfort level. I am not sure people will like to be told what to wear and what not to.'

In 2013, Jwala took a bold stand by pointing out unfair tactics used by an opposing team in the Badminton Premier League. As an icon player for the Delhi Smashers, she protested when a player was replaced against the rules, resulting in a half-hour match delay. Following this, the Badminton Association of India served Jwala with a show-cause notice. Despite the federation initially imposing a life ban, the Delhi High Court intervened and allowed her to continue playing.

She once told *The Hindustan Times*, 'I know I can come across as arrogant or unapproachable, but that's because I'm shy. Not many people know that about me. I seem unapproachable only because I don't know how to approach it! I don't know how to start a conversation, but I don't stop once I do. I like being private, but I do like having fun. The fun part everyone knows!' Jwala was similar to Hufrish, who stood up for her rights more than two decades ago. She was honoured with the Arjuna Award in 2011 for her contributions to the sport of badminton, a deserving recognition to a loyal servant of the game.

Subrahmanyam summed up her contributions aptly. 'It is a remarkable achievement by Jwala that she reminded the badminton world that doubles is also one of those important events which bring name and fame. That she was a champion in mixed doubles on the world stage, combined with Diju, was a significant chapter of her success story. Jwala is one of the unsung stars of Indian badminton, though rebellious sometimes, for she never hesitated to express herself against what she felt was wrong. A trendsetter in women's doubles for the likes of Ashwini to look far beyond.'

19

Ashwini Ponnappa: Silent Warrior

It has been hard work for Ashwini Ponnappa. She started, at a young age, in a state known for hockey, athletics, cricket, swimming – and Padukone. 'Prakash sir was the role model.' She was thrilled when she was chosen to be part of the Padukone Academy. 'It was prestigious.'

India's best trained at the Padukone Academy, and the competitive environment propelled Ponnappa's progress. Although her father was a hockey player, Ponnappa loved badminton. She was not even nine when she acquired her first badminton racquet.

From 2006 onwards, women's doubles has earned greater attention in Indian badminton circles. 'Women have received more recognition than men,' she pointed out. The 2010 Commonwealth Games gold was the game-changer despite the pair's craving for better coaching facilities. Funding from the government had increased, and it was a much-needed push for the game. In doubles, especially, the more you compete, the better you get since it depends on the combination between the two players.

Remembering the gold in 2010, Ponnappa said, 'We trained a lot. We were excited to do well, and I must say the support from the crowd went a long way.' It was a strange pair because Jwala was demonstrative on the court, and Ponnappa was calm. They combined well, complemented each other, and mostly executed their game plan. Jwala took the net, and Ponnappa, with her agility and retrieving abilities, covered the court at the back effectively.

Ponnappa initially hesitated about playing doubles but decided to do so because of her future and the team's requirements. 'I had no choice because I was selected for the national camp as a doubles player. It was upsetting when they made me stop playing the singles, but looking back, I guess it was the right decision. Once we won the Commonwealth Games, it seemed justified. We did well, luckily. I have enjoyed playing the doubles.'

Ponnappa achieved most of her success as a doubles partner with Jwala. The two won a bronze medal at the 2011 World Championships. Her first national title was as a doubles player in the sub-junior section.

Doubles is about understanding your partner. Your relationship with your partner is critical to your success. For Ponnappa, the success attained in Jwala's company was essential, but then she moved on to figure out how to play with other players.

'When you decide to part ways, it's always a challenging, nasty process. It's easier when the coach, the strategic mastermind, makes the decisions,' said Ponnappa in an interview with *Sportstar*, highlighting her decision to play with three partners in mixed doubles: K. Nandagopal, B. Sumeeth Reddy and now Satwik Rankireddy. 'If they were my decisions, it wouldn't have been easy. But now, no emotions are attached to the partners; it depends on what the coach says.'

It was at the suggestion of Gopi Chand that she had agreed to the changes. Gopi told the twenty-eight-year-old to play with Sindhu, instead of her regular partner Sikki Reddy, in the women's team quarterfinals against Japan in the 2018 Jakarta Asian Games.

'We are going in the right direction by having doubles for players from a very young age. We should start at under-16.

Under-19 is a little late because other countries focus on doubles at a younger age, so their defence and reflexes are swift,' Ponnappa observed.

In Subrahmanyam's opinion, 'The advent of Ponnappa had a bigger impact on Jwala than anyone else. Her partnership elevated even Jwala onto the international stage. Till then, Jwala and Shruti Kurien, her doubles partner for a long time, had been confined mostly to achievements in India and sometimes at the Asian level. But it was apparent that Jwala and Ponnappa evolved into one of the most formidable women's doubles combinations in world badminton due to the sheer weight of their achievements.'

Badminton has changed by leaps and bounds, with loads of doubles players – including Satwik Rankireddy and Chirag Shetty – breaking barriers and setting the bar high. 'We are on the right track. There are tremendous opportunities to play abroad at a very young age. There is no shortage of playing facilities. Bangalore has almost 4,000 courts. It sounds unbelievable. We can do better by streamlining the coaching system to a certain standard at the grassroots level.' Ponnappa acknowledged the support of the former players. Ami messages her regularly. Madhumita was the coach of the team. Manjusha has been a significant support. 'They are all wonderful women.'

She said in her association with Jwala, 'Vimal sir told me to give it a shot. Our game plan matched. We had to put in a lot of work. She took the net, and I took the backcourt. We travelled a lot and got along well despite our different personalities. I was the quieter one, and she talked, which was good. Over the years, Gopi also ensured that badminton got elevated to the front, and he did focus on the doubles. He certainly helped a lot.'

The way Ponnappa combined with Jwala on the court was a treat to watch. The court coverage, those stunning interceptions at the net, and how they set up those big smashes are now part of Indian badminton folklore.

Ponnappa's longevity saw her form a partnership with Tanisha Crasto, fourteen years younger than her. 'My body had gone through a lot and needed a break. I have to be a lot more mindful about how I treat it. I could have pushed myself, but I risk getting injured. So, I needed to step away from the National Championships. Tanisha understands that. But while I can't push myself like she can, there won't ever be a moment when she thinks I'm not training or giving anything less than my best.'

Ponnappa is a hard worker. It won't be that she'll be sitting around. There's a significant age gap between Ponnappa and Tanisha, so it's natural that they see things differently. She switches to being a mentor at times. While Tanisha is young, she can listen and learn. If she needs help, Ponnappa is always there. 'I enjoy her excitement,' Ponnappa praised Tanisha in an interview with *Sportstar*.

The 2024 Paris Olympics was Ponnappa's third appearance in the Olympics and Tanisha's debut. It helps Ponnappa that Tanisha is a quick learner. The thirty-four-year-old Ponnappa and Tanisha have hopes for the future.

20

Saina Nehwal: Epitome of Determination

SAINA NEHWAL WAS THE first Indian woman to command attention in a male-dominated sport. In 2012, she became the first Indian badminton player to win an Olympic medal in London. Her hard work accorded Saina the distinction of being counted among the greats in India.

Her dream was to make a name for herself as a karate kid. She was good at it too, but when her father, Harvir Singh, was transferred from Hissar to Hyderabad, life changed for Saina. Badminton replaced karate, and she adapted to a game which her mother, Usha, had represented at the state level.

Saina was eight when she took her first steps in badminton under coaches Nani Prasad, Arif and U. Bhaskar Babu. Saina made up for what she lacked in talent with determined hard work. To add variety to her game, she played a lot against boys. 'They have different shots, which helps you improve your defence,' she said.

'When I started, I didn't have any role models to look up to and say, 'I want to be world number one or be an Olympic medallist,' I hadn't seen anyone do that in badminton before me. I loved hard work. I could have been a more talented person. I needed to practice a lot. If a talented player is doing something a hundred times, I have to do it a thousand times. But I like hard work. My coaches liked my never-give-up attitude,' Saina said in an interview with *Sportstar*.

Her debut in the Olympics in Beijing in 2008 was a turning point in Saina's career. Gopi Chand has worked with her since 2006, and the transformation was remarkable. Saina defeated then world number 5 Wang Chen to reach the quarterfinals, where Indonesian star Maria Kristin proved the stumbling block for the Indian. But she had done enough to make the critics take notice of her potential.

Selector and coach Manjusha described Saina as a perfect example of an individual making the most of limited talent. 'I give more credit to Saina in women's badminton because she excelled when there was nobody to look up to. Her consistency and willpower were unheard of in that era: her capacity to work hard and the real power to beat the Chinese was exemplary. We have not witnessed that kind of self-belief.'

Saina left her contemporaries in awe with the hours spent on the court and in the gym. While others were pursuing their dreams, Saina was backing herself as the best. She practised eight to ten hours daily, punishing her body ahead of big tournaments. She had the passion to succeed like Padukone and the determination that marked the rise of players like Ami and Aparna.

Saina was genetically blessed with a muscular body, which worked well for her. Her mother was a sportswoman, and her father ensured her diet was taken care of as she made rapid strides on the national circuit. Her game was modelled on wearing down the opponent. Saina could last hours on the court, and her splendid footwork gave her a distinct advantage.

Gopi Chand concentrated on this strong athlete to give hope to Indian badminton. He turned Saina into an international player to reckon with. He paid full attention to Saina at his academy as Hyderabad gradually emerged as the country's hub of badminton.

Saina was the first to accept that she had to work harder than others to succeed, and she made no compromises regarding dedication. Her world revolved around her parents, coach and the game. Her contemporaries respected her for how she prepared every season – there were no distractions, parties, or movies. She would retire to her room and wait for the next day. These qualities helped her remain in the top five of the world for several years, challenging elite Chinese, Koreans and Indonesians players.

Manjusha remembers Saina fondly. 'Her court-craft was terrific. She would go on and on for hours to tire the opponents. She had a fantastic retrieving game. She used to smash also very hard. There were only a few shuttles that she would leave. And she could constantly smash from every corner and retrieve almost every shuttle.'

Saina could go on for long rallies and rarely got caught on the wrong foot. She had learnt the balance from watching Padukone. She had worked on the deception to fox her opponents with a sudden change of pace. The 2008 Beijing Olympics promoted her as the next big thing in Indian badminton. Appreciation came in the form of the Arjuna Award in 2009 and the prestigious Rajiv Gandhi Khel Ratna Award next year.

Titles came her way regularly, beginning with the Indonesian Open in 2009, when she became the first Indian to win a BWF Super Series event. It was followed by the India Open, which she won without dropping a game. The 2010 Commonwealth Games was a significant moment in her career, as she saved a match point against Malaysia's Wong Mew Choo to claim the gold. Saina was on song, and her dream had begun to take a glorious shape. She was ready for bigger deeds.

Saina, who won the national championships in 2007, 2011, 2013 and 2017, emerged as the best among India's women's badminton players. Her fourth-placed seeding at the Olympics in 2012 was an indication of the progress Saina had made, and she did not disappoint, overcoming Jie Yao of the Netherlands and Tine Baun of Denmark to set up a semifinal clash with the top-seeded Wang Yihan of China. Wang won in straight games.

'Unfortunately, I could not raise my game as the aftereffects of the viral fever took their full toll. Yihan realised I was not moving too well and hustled me around the court,' Nehwal said later. 'The lack of stamina saw me surrender without a fight. I was disappointed. I had gone to London to win the gold.'

Saina was up against China's Wang Xin in the play-off match for the bronze medal. She made history by default, as Wang had to retire at the start of the second game after winning the first. 'I was extremely surprised when it happened. I wanted to win my medal by defeating my opponent,' said Nehwal later.

'I was a bit rattled to see her in agony and went across to console her. But it was a special moment in my career when I won the Olympic bronze. It has always been my and my parents' dream since I joined badminton in 1999. Hard work, belief and some sacrifices made it possible,' she said.

Her progress was steady even as Indian badminton witnessed the emergence of Sindhu, a precocious talent, also from Hyderabad. In their first meeting, Saina beat Sindhu in the final of the 2014 India Open.

In 2014, Saina had a spat with the badminton authorities when she was dropped from the Indian team for the Asian Games in Incheon because of fitness issues. She had opted out of the Commonwealth Games the same year earlier because of an injury and could not convince the selectors.

In April 2015, Nehwal became world number 1, the first Indian to claim that honour. Saina was over the moon. 'It's still unbelievable that I am the world number 1. When I see myself in the rankings chart, I can't believe it. It's a big achievement that every player dreams of. We saw Li Xuerui there for a long time and now there will be a change in the name. I think it's all because of the performances I am showing,' she said after reaching the pinnacle of her career. She also played in the final of the All-England Open, but Carolina Marin, the Olympic champion, proved too strong for Saina.

'Badminton is fitness, speed and endurance,' was her observation then. It was beginning to challenge her dominance now. She went down in the second round of the 2016 Rio Olympics and paid the price for playing with an injured knee.

Saina parted with Gopi Chand to make things work and found a new coach in Vimal. In August 2014, unhappy with her continued failure against Li Xuerui, she contemplated quitting badminton after losing in the World Championship quarterfinals. 'I was tired of losing to the same player again and again (eighth in succession). But Vimal Sir told me that there was nothing wrong with my game. He pointed out areas in my game that needed improvement,' she said later.

In an interview with *Sportstar*, Vimal disclosed, 'I suggested that she bring in some more variations from the back of the court. Then she could bring in those faster, deceptive clearances from the sides, a straight flick down the line and cross-drops. So, I suggested that she mix it up well – the net tumble with the cross-drops,' said Vimal.

Eight years after her first Commonwealth Games in Delhi, she repeated the feat in 2018 with a memorable victory against Sindhu. The same year she won the bronze medal at the 2018 Asian Games. She defeated Ratchanok Intanon of Thailand in the quarterfinals before losing to the ultimate champion, Tai Tzu-ying of Taiwan in the semifinals. For the bronze medal, she overcame Indonesia's Gregoria Mariska Tunjung.

Saina made a momentous decision in 2018 to marry Parupalli Kashyap, a fellow badminton player. The private ceremony in Hyderabad surprised the badminton fraternity. Three years later, slowed down by a knee injury, she failed to qualify for the Tokyo Olympics. Her twelve-year-long career, decorated with twenty-four international titles, eleven in Super Series, witnessed a modest end.

As analysed by Subrahmanyam, 'To her credit, Saina has earned a reputation of being a fighter over the years, never one to give up even under extreme pressure on a badminton court. That is perhaps in her genes, which come from her parents, who are from Haryana! In her day, Saina was a complete player who used to take time to read the opponent, and once she had done it, Saina was just too good with a range of strokes, which were a delight to the connoisseurs.'

She is also the only Indian to have won at least one medal in every BWF major – the World Championships, the World Junior Championships – and that most precious bronze medal at the Olympics. Saina placed herself in elite company, winning medals at the Olympics, World Championships, Commonwealth Games, Asian Championships and the Asian Games. She is only the second woman to do so after former Chinese player Li Lingwei.

Sanjay Sharma recalled, 'Saina is the best female player India has produced in any sport. Her contribution is huge. She was not a born talent but pushed herself to the limits through hard work and used her brain well. Her determination was exemplary. When she won the Philippines Open at the age of seventeen, Gopi warned her that she might encounter some formidable Chinese opponents soon. Saina responded, *Aane do sir, maarungi main*' (let them come, I will beat them). Such confidence was unheard in Indian badminton.'

In recognition of her path-breaking contributions to the game, President Droupadi Murmu invited Saina to the 'Her Story, My Story' lecture series featuring women Padma awardees. Saina, a Padma Shri and Padma Bhushan, delivered a talk at the Rashtrapati Bhavan Cultural Centre in early July 2024, and shared moments from her iconic journey.

21

P. V. Sindhu: The Swift Conqueror

SPORTS AND PUSARLA VENKATA Sindhu are deeply intertwined. Her parents – distinguished volleyball players – had a significant influence on Sindhu's life. An early incident from her life gives an insight into her ambitions.

Speaking with Forbes, Sindhu revealed an anecdote from childhood to indicate what contributed to her becoming a sportsperson. She picked up her father, P. V. Ramana's visiting card and struck off his name to overwrite her own. 'He was a champion, and I wanted to be one,' Sindhu laughed. She did become one, becoming the first Indian to win back-to-back Olympic medals – silver at Rio in 2016 and bronze at Tokyo in 2021.

For Sindhu, 2012 was a path-breaking phase of her career. At seventeen, the lanky shuttler shocked the London Olympics gold medallist Li Xuerui of China 21–19, 9–21, 21–16 in the quarterfinals at the China Masters Super Series badminton tournament. 'She was the Olympic champion then, and I beat her. That surely was the turning point for me,' she said in an interview.

Ramana has played a massive role in Sindhu's journey. He would wake up at 3:30 a.m. and prepare for the daily practice routine – driving 30 km one way. 'She would sleep off in the car,' revealed Ramana, who was a reputed volleyball player and an Arjuna awardee.

Gachibowli, the training place, was worth the pain that Ramana and Sindhu undertook daily. To avoid the tiresome journey, Sindhu began staying back at the academy, to return home only in the evening. Then she would stay at the academy and come home for weekends. It was tough. Things eased when Ramana bought a house close to the academy, a five-minute drive. At no point, did Ramana and Sindhu relax. 'It was unrelenting,' Ramana had recalled. For Sindhu, it was remarkable support from her parents, who took voluntary retirement from their government job in the railways to concentrate on her career.

Gopi Chand, who set up an academy to train promising players of Indian badminton, was the inspiration for Sindhu. In 2009, she showed definite signs of attaining greater heights when she won a bronze at the sub-junior Asian Badminton Championships. The next year she claimed a silver in the International Badminton Challenge in Iran in 2010. Gopi was beginning to see a champion in Sindhu, who also backed herself.

Sindhu ranks among the greatest athletes produced by India. She won a bronze at the World Championships in 2013 and 2014 followed by a silver each at the World Championships in 2017 and 2018. Her focus on the game made a big impression on the followers when she missed her sister's (Divya) wedding in December 2012 because she was committed to participate in the Modi International Grand Prix Gold in Lucknow. 'Yeah, I will be missing her wedding. I can't help it now having reached the final,' said Sindhu at the event. 'I will try to win the tournament and give it as a gift to her.' In the final, Sindhu whipped Gregoria Mariska 21–13, 21–14, to the delight of her elder sister.

The silver at the Rio Olympics was in keeping with her amazing consistency even though, according to her well-wishers, she was performing below her expectations. The final against Spain's Carolina Marin was well contested. Marin won 19–21, 21–12, 21–15 as she became the first European woman to win the Olympics badminton gold.

Remembering the final in *Sportstar*, Sindhu said, 'The best part of Rio was obviously getting a medal for the country and standing on the podium. Nothing can beat that or be as good as that. I was on cloud nine. It took a while for that achievement to sink in. After that, I gained a lot of confidence and motivation game-wise, on court and off court. In the final, it was anybody's game. I was leading 11–10 in the decider when Carolina Marin took a couple of points and led overall to clinch the gold. At the end of it, one player must win and the other loses. I have taken it in a very positive way. I had to be happy. Yes, if you lose, you will be upset. But the feeling I got when I was standing on the podium was different – I won the silver and not that I lost the gold!'

Sindhu is candid, 'When I started playing badminton, I never dreamt of playing in the Olympics. The effort and focus then was on becoming a good player who can win titles at the national level. But after I joined the Gopi Chand Academy, I started looking at things differently. Slowly my goals started changing with every passing month. I am glad that I am in the best academy and under the best coach, Gopi Sir. I am fortunate to have someone like him as my coach.'

Gopi is a hard taskmaster. Discipline was the key as he concentrated on Sindhu. It was tough for Sindhu as Gopi denied her access to mobile phones and tablets. Sindhu understood she had to make these adjustments. At the end of the Rio Olympics, she said, 'When you have set a big goal, like winning an Olympic medal, you have to be prepared for these kinds of small sacrifices. I didn't have any issue with this, and I am glad – I repeat – I had a coach who was so committed to ensuring my success on the biggest stage. For instance, now I have already had enough chocolates and ice creams after coming home. I was not allowed to have them for close to three months in the run-up to the Olympics.'

Losses in the finals did hurt Sindhu but she finally met her goal in 2019 with a victory over Nozomi Okuhara in the World Championship final. The first ever Indian badminton player to have won a World Championship. The Sindhu–Marin rivalry has been one of the most celebrated in badminton with the Spaniard leading the rivalry 12–6 ahead of the Paris Olympics.

Since 2022, Sindhu has had fitness issues. The 2020 gold at the Commonwealth Games was in keeping with the form even though she played with an ankle injury after the quarter final stage. The stress led to a five-month leave from the game and it hindered her progress. Sindhu was forced to change her coach in 2024 and the support staff before she could regain her touch.

'I wonder why she has started playing defensively. I have sent a message to Prakash (Padukone) to check on this change in her game. Prakash was kind enough to say he would consider the suggestion,' said Sanjay Sharma in a critical analysis of Sindhu's new style.

Ramana and Vijaya have been outstanding pillars in Sindhu's success. 'I think they have proved once again, with their unstinting support, that for any athlete to make it big, the first support system is at home. Unless parents wholeheartedly extend their fullest co-operation, it is extremely difficult to make it big in sports. I am fortunately blessed with such parents. Their caring and understanding of what it takes to make a champion, and the readiness to make so many sacrifices is remarkable,' she said in praise of her parents.

For long, there was talk of an undercurrent of acrimony between Sindhu and Saina. Both hailing from the same city added fuel to the fire as the media hunted for opportunities to highlight the friction between the two. Sindhu clarified her stand, 'Oh! She (Saina) has achieved so much. I admire her fighting spirit, as she never gives any easy points. Since she trains at a different place, we tend to meet only during tournaments. There also, but for exchanging pleasantries and casual enquiries about the players we are likely to meet, there is no time for long, serious talks. Both of us have our priorities and goals to achieve. Otherwise, the rest is all speculation.'

Sindhu's early days in the circuit resulted from her dominating personality – both on and off the court, observed Subrahmanyam. 'The tall and lanky shuttler became synonymous with her awesome smashes, again perhaps picking up a few things from her parents, who both represented India in volleyball. There is very little to separate Saina and Sindhu regarding the court movements. The big difference can be that Saina often pulled off sensational wins while Sindhu faltered in the tense moments of a decider – perhaps caught in the dilemma of whether to attack or defend.'

Born on 5 July 1995, in Hyderabad, Sindhu is the first Indian woman to grab a gold at the BWF Championships. She achieved the feat in 2019. She has received honours like the Padma Shree in 2015, Khel Ratna in 2016 and the Padma Bhushan in 2020. She acknowledges the love she gets from her fans. A medal at the Paris Olympics could add to her stature – three in a row.

22

Behind the Scenes: Unsung Heroes of Indian Badminton

THE BACKSTAGE WORKERS HAVE always been the backbone of any sport that excelled on the biggest stage. True, there are champions, but then there are those who toil tirelessly to provide support from the opposite court or alongside. With the selfless contributions of these unsung players, the game could progress in the era of their active participation at any level.

Most champions have sparring partners, especially in games where the competition is intense. Boxing and wrestling partners hardly get mentioned when the champion climbs the podium. Similar foot soldiers in badminton strive to be in the company of the stars by becoming their partners or opponents during training sessions.

For national players like Ajay Kanwar, Vikram Bisht, and Malvinder Dhillon, it was a matter of pride when Padukone requested them to organise training sessions before the team's departure or at camps. The benefits were mutual. The lesser-known players would look to learn some finer points, while the higher-ranked stars gained from the severe sessions aimed at keeping them on their toes.

The coaches would set specific goals for the season, and the practice sessions would have to maintain a certain degree of competitive integrity. For Bisht and Kanwar, the sessions with Padukone would mean an education. 'We looked forward to training with him,' Bisht said. Kanwar would be equally excited, and he always marvelled at Padukone's devotion to his game.

For Bisht, some of the memorable times came when hosting Padukone. 'I can't forget his simplicity, the attire and how he would be happy to sleep on the floor. I have not seen a humbler champion.'

Dhillon has fond memories of Padukone. He had begun playing badminton at an open court outside his home in west Delhi. Rains and winds would bring his badminton to a stop, and it was much later that Dhillon discovered badminton was an indoor game. To play indoors, he and his friend would cycle down to Bal Bhawan, 15 km away, where they got one shuttle for three training days. 'It was worth it and great fun,' Dhillon remembered.

Amazingly, Dhillon managed to keep his love for badminton a secret from his father until one fine morning when the newspapers reported him winning the state junior title in 1968. His father encouraged him to play more, and the following year, Dhillon won the national title, his only one, at Calcutta. And what a feat it was as he overcame Padukone in the final.

Before the Calcutta nationals, an incident greatly impacted Dhillon. A senior player had stopped a newspaper reporter from publishing Dhillon's photo after he won the Delhi state title. It hurt Dhillon when the senior said he didn't deserve media recognition. The senior challenged Dhillon to win a national title and earn the privilege of having his photo published.

Dhillon remembered these words when he arrived in Calcutta. He did not drop a game on the way to the final, where he beat Padukone straight. For an unseeded player, it was a magnificent achievement against an opponent like Padukone, considered unbeatable in the domestic circuit. Dhillon won 15–4, 15–11, and more than the triumph, he remembered the tight hug that Padukone gave him.

Dhillon also recalled touching the legendary Suresh Goel's feet before the final. 'His blessings worked wonders for me,' Dhillon said. It was also the beginning of a lasting friendship with Padukone. Padukone makes it a point to meet Dhillon whenever he visits Delhi.

Dhillon suffered a collarbone injury soon after the Calcutta win, and his junior circuit ended. He continued to play and could never forget the experience of watching players like Goel, Khanna and T. N. Seth in his later years. 'Goel was an exceptional player. His opponents did not know where to hit the shuttle because he was everywhere. I became a good rally player because of watching him and Prakash.'

Seth was the national champion for three years, beginning in 1956. He enriched the Indian badminton circuit with his all-round game and was a hard nut to crack on the court. Opponents often wondered at his fitness levels and smooth court movements. In his way, he served Indian badminton with distinction. Dipankar Bhattacharjee emulated Seth by winning the title in 1993, 1994 and 1995. Satish Bhatia, Dipu Ghosh, and George Thomas were all one-time winners of the national title, but they came back to challenge the better-ranked opponents.

Shobha and Rafia Latif claimed the national crown once each in 1971 and 1972, like Radhika Bose in 1982. P. V. V. Lakshmi distinguished herself by winning in 1994 and 1995. Aditi Mutatkar's title came in 2010 after hard work on the circuit. The women's circuit grew in competition over the years, but the absence of top stars often took the sheen away from the tournaments.

Uday Pawar was another dedicated player who looked for success in doubles by partnering with Leroy. Apart from the Ghosh brothers, this pair promised to make an impact at the highest level. The talented Pawar made a splendid debut in the 1976 senior nationals when he went past four seeded players but succumbed to the guiles of Padukone in the final. Pawar's superb show had earned him a slot in the Indian team for the first-ever World Championships held in Sweden.

Pawar and D'Sa admire the success attained by the pair of Satwiksairaj Rankireddy and Chirag Shetty. They lived up to expectations by winning bronze in the 2022 World Championships after the bronze by Jwala and Ashwini Ponnappa in 2011. The pair of Satwik and Chirag added the French Open gold with a magnificent win over Lee Jhe Huei and Yang Po Hsuan of Chinese Taipei. It was one of the most significant triumphs by an Indian pair in doubles.

The focus may always be on the champions, but they also acknowledge the efforts of these backstage warriors who gave them the competition that brought a sense of achievement when they won a medal. It is not always about the winners. Even losers contribute by getting the best out of the champions.

23

Game Changers: Evolution of Badminton Leagues in India

THE INDIAN PREMIER LEAGUE (IPL) changed the way fans followed sports in India. After hockey and football, cricket has always been the most popular sport, and the IPL established it as the leader in terms of commercial returns. The revenue it generated for the Board of Control for Cricket in India (BCCI) became a case study for the other national sports federations on successful administration. There was financial security for the players and the different stakeholders, leading to a mushrooming of franchise leagues in other popular sports.

The IPL was not the first sporting league. In 2005, the Indian Hockey Federation (IHF) approved the Premier Hockey League (PHL), making it India's first competitive hockey league. The league gained widespread attention and support from fans and the media. Despite ending in 2008, the PHL significantly elevated the sport by adding glamour and media coverage, turning hockey players into household names.

The following sporting innovation was launched in 2007 when cricket great Kapil Dev lent his support to the Indian Cricket League (ICL). The move generated a lot of interest as some of the world's best cricketers participated in the ICL, which, however, faded away after one more edition as the BCCI took a strict view and created obstacles for the organisers. The lack of venues was the main reason the ICL discontinued its expansion plans.

There was a wave of professionalism in Indian sports, and badminton was not to fall behind. The increase in sponsorship for the players was a sign of changing times. Players were happy to receive top-class equipment for free. Having a steady supply of shuttles, racquets, and comfortable shoes on the court was considered a privilege even by the top-ranked players. Times changed when the government categorised badminton as a priority sport, and then there was no looking back.

Some notable sporting leagues included the Premier Handball League, I-League, Pro Kabaddi, Hockey India League, Ultimate Table Tennis, Prime Volleyball League, Ultimate Kho Kho, and Women's Premier League. The focus was on making the players self-sustaining since public sector jobs had dried up and the youngsters needed motivation to pursue a career in sports.

The number of tournaments with prize money on offer went a long way in boosting the profile of badminton. The fact that it was a sport not impacted by doping was a massive advantage for the game over others as sports federations battled with the vexed issues of doping and age fudging. The Badminton Federation of India (BFI) faced problems related to age manipulation, but it overcame them.

For Indian players, foreign exposure was rare, and the players felt out of place when leaving for tournaments abroad. It was a disheartening process where the players had to travel to Delhi from their hometowns, often by train and bus, when applying for visas. Even their accommodation in Delhi was on their own, with stalwarts like Padukone, at times, staying at the homes of friends from the fraternity.

There were other challenges, too, like getting used to the shuttles. They would train primarily with Indian shuttles and get the Yonex brand for practice only when they travelled overseas for tournaments. Players often came to Delhi and prayed for the visas to arrive on time. There have been instances when they received the visa hours before the departure.

The situation changed when the BFI implemented a professional approach initiated by the former BAI. The All-India ranking tournaments were organised at different levels, including sub-junior (under 13 and 15), junior (under 17 and 19) and senior categories. These tournaments took place in small centres nationwide to attract local talent and establish infrastructure in various areas. At the state and zonal levels, these tournaments served as the basis for selecting players for the national teams.

Badminton also progressed through support from some institutional teams, where players earned employment as financial security. Organizations like the Reserve Bank of India, Life Insurance Corporation of India, Indian Railways, Air Force, Food Corporation of India, BSNL Sports Board, Airports Authority of India, Ordnance Factory, Department of Atomic Energy, Employees State Insurance Corporation and Air India showed the way for Indian Oil and Oil and Natural Gas Corporation to employ players at various posts.

By engaging foreign coaches, the BFI ensured modern thinking in badminton, and the players adapted too. The general feeling was that it helped their image if the game remained clean, and the results attracted sponsors. Gopi Chand looked at it with positive intent when he credited the PBL for the phenomenal steps the game took to invite more significant participation in domestic tournaments.

'The sport has jumped in all parameters. Prakash (Padukone) sir played leagues in Denmark, Vimal (Kumar) played in the UK, others have been to France, I have played in Germany, and today, we host the biggest league in the world (PBL). Things have changed. We have (Carolina) Marin coming here to play, Viktor (Axelsen) coming here to play,' Gopi had observed when interacting with youngsters at an IDBI Federal Young

Champs programme. 'The tournaments or the leagues happening in those countries over the years had to change their programmes because India was hosting the league. That is a (huge) change. The earnings of top players have gone up. They encourage a whole set of people to take the sport forward.'

The rise in number of participants in doubles earned a special mention from Gopi Chand. 'In 2008–2009, the doubles events at the state championships in Maharashtra had to be scrapped as there was not much participation from women shuttlers. We did not have eight entries to fill a draw. We had to cancel the doubles because of a lack of entries. That is where the numbers were, and we had real trouble. In 2019, we had around 3,000 entries for the tournament. That's the jump you have seen. The numbers have consistently grown. When I was playing, we had three courts during competitions; today, you have ten to twenty courts. There are draws and qualifications in juniors and sub-juniors, so that says it all.'

The Indian Badminton League (IBL) – launched in 2013 – significantly impacted the game. It rapidly grew in stature and brought some of the biggest names in world badminton. The first season of the IBL comprised six teams, and Hyderabad Hotshots won the competition. The event was put on hold until 2016, when it was brought back with a new name – Premier Badminton League. It had made steady progress, but COVID-19 halted the league.

As Gopi Chand pointed out, badminton was a game where men's singles players dominated the national scene. Natekar, Padukone, Khanna, Modi, and Suresh Goel were better known for their exploits than the women players. The arrival of Saina and Sindhu changed all that, and the sponsors had new avenues to explore. Elsewhere, Sania Mirza emerged as the face of women's tennis in India, and Leander Paes became the finest individual after Vijay Amritraj and Ramesh Krishnan. For Saina and Sindhu to make a place for themselves – in a field of fierce competitors in wrestling, athletics, boxing, archery and chess – was the giant boost badminton benefited from.

Sindhu was the biggest draw for badminton. At the last PBL auction in 2019, she and Tai Tzu Ying of Chinese Taipei fetched ₹77 lakh each from their respective franchises. It was the best advertisement for badminton, where women players were attracting bids higher than some male players. Seventy-four Indian players earned a slot to play in different PBL teams in that edition.

The leagues recognised the badminton fraternity, where youngsters came with high hopes but ran into high training costs. Not everyone could afford private coaching, and they needed a financial boost to pursue their love for the game with self-respect. 'The players don't have the time and the reach to go and seek sponsorship. They have to concentrate on the game. Badminton is an expensive sport, and it can be very tough if you don't have a sponsor to back your dreams,' said Kanwar, now a coach with RISE, a state-of-the-art academy in Noida.

Badminton had yet to see much money. The cream of the world came to India. The exposure helped the Indian youngsters. So many of them got to see these elite professionals, travel with the them, watch them up close, and learn from players from Korea, Malaysia, and Indonesia. They were a mystery, and the players interacted with some legends. How they trained, prepared for matches, their diet and a lot more. It came from the league. In tournaments, you would see them only on the court. In leagues, players lived with them. Someone like Carolin Marin was one of the players who came to understand the game best only after playing in the IBL. Hailing from Spain, she realised her potential to the extent that she became the best woman player in the world.

The architect of the IBL was Akhilesh Das Gupta. As president of the BFI, he had a vision which was the betterment of the players. He had the will, the money and the political backing to undertake this excellent venture. Das single-handedly created the platform for the league. For many, it was not a commercially viable sport, but he wanted to make the players rich. Das was to badminton what Jagmohan Dalmiya was to cricket – bringing huge money to the sport that attracted more to consider a badminton career.

Maharashtra Badminton Association initially wanted to do a national-level badminton league, with recognition from the Badminton Association of India. However, their budget and plans were not enough to invite top international athletes, so it would have been a ₹50-lakh affair with almost all Indian players. Saina Nehwal had not won an Olympic medal, and Indian badminton didn't have global stars then.

It was the idea of Ashish Chadha, a former sports journalist and national-level badminton player, that marked a significant turning point. His company, Sporty Solutionz Private Limited, presented a highly lucrative proposal. This proposal, which was readily accepted by Akhilesh Das, paved the way for the league's launch.

The financial aspects of the league were substantial. The BAI was set to receive over ₹10 crore in license fees and revenue share over five years, with a commitment of ₹1 crore for the first year. The league, launched as the IBL in 2013, boasted top international stars, including the then-world number. 1 Lee Chong Wei, Danish, Spanish, and Indonesian players. Notably, China and Japan did not allow their players to participate in the league.

In the run-up to the league, differences cropped up between Sporty and the BAI. The first bone of contention was Yonex, which had absolute equipment rights for any and all tournaments under the BAI. But Sporty Solutionz had acquired all the rights for the league.

Yonex came on board, and Chadha had to accept the deal. However, the BAI terminated the contract following differences related to sharing the finances. Chadha, however, was awarded compensation later, and the league was called the Premier Badminton League.

Gopi Chand played a vital role in the success of the IBL's first season. Experts widely believed that in its infancy, the league missed Himanta Biswa Sarma's presence and ability to understand the situation and issues. He has since guided the game with an eye on the future.

Reflecting on the league, Kanwar noted, 'Star Sports played a big part. They took the game to the drawing room of the sports lovers. Badminton was hardly a spectator sport because there was no television. Camera work created magic for the viewers. Television played a huge role because former players explained the game's nuances, and badminton created many followers among the youth. The government had done its bit to keep the game going, but the league brought the money for them to prosper.'

As in the IPL, where state-level players could compete with and against world-class stars, the young players gained a lot from the badminton league because of their access to foreigners. As Ajay pointed out, it was easier to manage the foreign players who were far more professional and realised their responsibilities better. 'Look at Satwiksairaj (Rankireddy). We can call him a product of the league where he learnt to hone his skills in doubles and formed a fantastic partnership with Chirag (Shetty). Even Lakshya (Sen) made laudable progress because of the experience he gained in playing the league. Lakshya was picked as a junior and rose to great heights,' said Kanwar.

The popularity of the league meant greater participation of the other stakeholders. Sponsorship took a giant leap in prize money, and the players backed themselves by wanting to test themselves on the professional platform. The game received broad support to emerge as a commercially viable game. The visibility was crucial because badminton became India's most popular sport after cricket and football.

The increased media coverage and full-page advertisements featuring badminton stars marked a significant transformation for the sport. In the past, even the national championships struggled to earn decent space in the newspapers, and features and interviews of badminton stars were rare. However, the notable presence of players like Sindhu, Saina, Lakshya, Satwik and Shetty greatly contributed to the efforts of the BFI, elevating the sport to the stature it deserved. The awarding of the Arjuna Award to Sen and H. S. Prannoy in 2022 further confirmed that badminton was on the right track.

24

State of the Shuttle: Navigating the Currents of Indian Badminton

AJAY KANWAR, A FORMER national player active during Padukone's time, made an astonishing claim that Noida had 'One hundred courts in a radius of five kilometres!'

His academy, Raising Impact Through Sports Education & Excellence (RISE), has built on badminton's immense popularity in the wake of players like Sindhu, Saina, Sen, Kidambi, Prannoy, Praneeth and the doubles pair of Satwik Saireddy and Chirag Shetty, making it big in the international circuit.

Each time an Indian badminton player achieved international success, there was a surge in demand from parents who wanted their children to receive proper training. Badminton academies expanded nationwide, and the number of retired players transitioning into coaching roles increased significantly. Badminton courts were consistently occupied throughout the week as the sport gained popularity among those seeking recreational activities. The sport's non-combative nature, coupled with the absence of doping, made it an ideal choice for casual players.

Badminton is doing well compared to other sports. The facilities have improved, and the opportunities are aplenty at every level. Badminton has the most significant number of registered players, followed by table tennis. 'It reflects the popularity of badminton,' observed Bisht, a former player and coach at his academy at the Siri Fort Sports Complex.

These days, a state championship attracts at least a thousand entries in each of the three categories – sub-junior, junior and senior. 'Since the facilities have improved and India has shown great results at the international level, the expectations have also grown,' noted Arif.

The government stepped in when it became apparent that the sport required significant financial support to grow. Players had requested better equipment and courts to improve their abilities, and the government was happy to assist. The Sports Ministry and the Sports Authority of India provided the necessary boost. Gopi Chand played a central role in the committee, which was responsible for planning and implementing ideas to raise badminton standards in the country.

In 2014, the government introduced the Target Olympics Podium Scheme (TOPS), which aimed to give the top athletes the support they needed to win Olympic medals. According to the SAI, 'We revamped the scheme in April 2018 to establish a technical support team for managing the TOPS athletes and providing holistic support. The fully functional scheme has extended all requisite support to probable athletes identified for the Olympic Games and Paralympic Games, including foreign training, international competition, equipment and coaching camp, besides a monthly stipend of ₹ 50,000 for each athlete.' It came as a boon for the badminton players.

The impact of good administration by the BAI was seen in Manipur's sensational showing in the fifth Interstate-Inter Zonal National Championships at Pune (2022–2023) when it finished runner-up. It was a fantastic development in the badminton fraternity since the state had no culture of playing badminton. Hockey, football and boxing were the primary disciplines that brought Manipur to India's sporting map. Their success in badminton had taken the nation by surprise.

Manipur led 2–0 in the final against Petroleum Sports Promotion Board, but inexperience cost them the title. Manipur had claimed the bronze in the 2018 edition of the championships. Maisnam Meiraba Luwang made Manipur proud with his performance against the fancied Kidambi Srikanth in the second round of the 84th Senior National Badminton Championships. He lost 19–21, 21–18, 17–21 as the former world number 1 brought out his talent to survive against the inspired Maisnam.

In an interview with Shahid Judge of *Scroll*, Maisnam explained why his state did so well: 'Lots of Manipuris have started to go outside the state – some to Bangalore and some to Hyderabad. They're getting to train under better facilities. That is the main reason. I may have influenced it a little bit. I first left in 2012 to play in an under-13 ranking event in Bangalore at the Padukone Academy. We saw what that place was like, and my father asked if I could train there. They had a twenty-one-day camp, and I was selected. I've been there since 2013.'

Indian badminton is in its healthiest state. As of 2024 there are more than twenty players across categories in the top 100 in the world, most of them participating in fifteen-odd tournaments in a season, which is a phenomenal rise of the game. 'Today, you have seniors and juniors playing tournaments on their own. That concept didn't exist in my time. You had to be part of the Indian team, or you were not part of the touring squads,' observed Bisht.

The rising number of youngsters playing in tournaments overseas also confirmed the growth of badminton in India. The abundance of academies was due to the interest in the lucrative leagues. It is well-known that most players have emerged from these academies. 'Without academies, the game would not prosper,' noted Bisht. Some experts, however, believe badminton has yet to grow at the expected rates. 'Thirty years ago, students in government schools participated more actively,' claims Sudhanshu Fadnis from RISE Academy.

'Badminton academies are essentially business ventures, and there is nothing wrong with that, but the structure for school badminton is missing. There has to be a process. School championship is the first step. Khelo India Youth Games, a government initiative, is helping identify talent. As a school champion, you get admission to a college, which is the youngsters' incentive. If a player wins in the Khelo India Youth Games, the BAI should recognise it. That individual should get the status of a national champion,' said Fadnis.

After the launch of the Khelo India district centre, the scheme has gained momentum. Each district can have a local coach for the badminton fraternity, and ₹ 5 lakh is allotted to each centre every year. 'The state governments can help. The grassroots has to be created by the local strength and not by the federation,' said Kanwar. 'Dedicated coaching for boys and girls (under-15, 17 and 19) will make the difference.'

The involvement of recently retired players has ensured the coaching methods at the junior level are in tune with the times. 'We have to pay these former players so they can sustain themselves and do their job sincerely,' stresses Kanwar.' The best thing we can do is use them for the junior teams. I have seen the top former players from China and Indonesia travel with the junior players more than with the senior squad,' Kanwar stressed.

TOPS is the key to the future success of badminton. However, Kanwar points out that though TOPS has an exceptional team of coaches, they focus only on the forty players under contract. At the lower level, the game remains expensive to pursue. 'It costs ₹ 2,000 per box of shuttles. There is no shortage in TOPS, but it is hard to meet the expenses at the state-level academy. A total of 3.5 lakh is spent monthly on shuttles, where state-level players are engaged. Things have become better, yes, but there is room for improvement,' Kanwar emphasised. Badminton is a costly sport. There are courts and equipment fees to handle. He reveals that many parents take out risky bank loans to support their kids' dreams of having a badminton career.

There has been a drastic change in how players prepare for big tournaments. In the past, most of the camps were conducted in Patiala. The coaches were former players – some would have never played at a high level. It has changed now. The players go to different academies. Some even have personal coaches. 'It is good to see a hundred players practising in one place. It is a great sport to be a professional coach. There is a surge, and we need to recognise it,' said former player Bisht.

In a step seen as a massive boost to India's game, the BAI established the National Centre of Excellence (NCE) at Guwahati in 2023. It is the infrastructure needed to modernise badminton in the country. The centre boasts 14 courts, a 4,000-square-foot gymnasium with modern fitness equipment, a state-of-the-art 60-bed hostel for players, and a 2,000-square-foot physiotherapy facility.

The NCE will build a core base of players and coaches to train them. The BAI deserves credit for bringing in foreign coaches, such as the renowned Mulyo Handoyo of Indonesia, to look after the development of the singles players. Russia's Ivan Sozonov and Korea's Park Tae-Sang, both international stars, have been recruited to develop a coaching team. These developments are expected to be game changers for the future of badminton in India.

'Badminton has come a long way. It is in a much better state than it was in my youth. In the 1960s and early 1970s, Rudy Hartono of Indonesia made badminton much faster and more physically demanding than it used to be. Now, it has become even more physically demanding. Still, badminton's quality has dipped from the spectator's point of view compared to the time of Natekar and Erland Kops. These people used to go for the lines. Now, badminton is much more defensive. Players play down the centre of the court; rarely do they go for the line. I call it the Sunil Gavaskar frame of mind. The player first wants to ensure they don't lose, and then they think about winning. So, a more defensive mindset has come into play in badminton over the years,' stresses Nadkarni.

Acknowledgements

WE EMBARKED ON THIS journey to celebrate the unique and irreplaceable contributions of Indians who are international stars and unsung heroes. Through their unwavering participation, each of them has played a pivotal role in keeping the game of badminton alive. Their roles in this project are invaluable.

The inspiration came from veteran player and sportswriter Shirish Nadkarni's iconic work *Courting Success*. We have benefited immensely from Nadkarni's writings on each aspect of the game. He gave us precious time to provide priceless insight into the game's history. Furthermore, he has generously allowed us to reproduce rare and priceless pictures from his private collection.

At the outset, we thank our editor, Paul Vinay Kumar, for his monumental patience and understanding as we repeatedly missed the deadline.

We thank Krishan Chopra for his unwavering faith and trust in our effort.

V. V. Subrahmanyam of *The Hindu and Sportstar* is integral to this book. His insightful writing on badminton and interactions with modern stars laid the foundation for us to build upon. He also contributed by providing pictures he took when covering tournaments.

We want to express our sincere gratitude to Rakesh Rao of *The Hindu and Sportstar*. His generous introduction to the individuals featured in this story has enriched our narrative and added a layer of authenticity that words cannot fully describe.

We thank former sports journalist Udita Dutta of Artsmith Concepts and Visions for facilitating the procurement of pictures from the Badminton Association of India.

Sanjay Sharma, one of the most read writers on badminton, instantly agreed to share his experience.

Abhijeet Kulkarni, an acknowledged expert on the game, was always there to add his wisdom and guide us.

Pullela Gopi Chand, one of the game's greats, was very kind in writing the foreword.

We sincerely appreciate the support from the players who happily shared their time and stories with us. Their contributions have enriched this project beyond measure.

We would also like to thank Ayon Sengupta, editor of *Sportstar*, for providing us with invaluable images for the book. *The Hindu* and *Sportstar* have been our principal sources of information. This group of publications is known for its specialised sports coverage, and we have benefited immensely from their work.

Finally, we are indebted to Sunanda Lokapally's encouragement. Her unwavering backing is why this book has finally taken shape, and we are grateful for her belief in our endeavour.

Index

2012 London Olympics, The, 4, 157, 174
2016 Rio Olympics, The, 4, 186

Ahmad, Fazil, 60, 68, 110
Ahuja, Devinder, 61, 139
Allahabad, 41–42
Ambala, 41, 99, 102
Amethi, 85–86
Amritsar, 11, 24–25, 27–28, 30
Andhra Pradesh, 50, 61
Apte, Sarojini, 35
Apte sisters, The, 4, 35
Apte, Sunila, 35
Arif, Syed Mohammed (*also* Arif Saab), 49–56, 150–151, 153, 156, 171, 173, 182, 206
Arjuna Award, The, 39, 41, 154, 177, 184, 204
Athletics, 29, 38, 104, 178, 201

Badminton Association of India (BAI), 5, 31, 50, 60, 65–68, 95, 109–110, 133, 157, 175–176, 199, 202–203, 206, 208–209
Bafna, Sudha, 140
Bagga, Rajeev, 56, 62, 131
Bangalore, 62, 67, 82, 110, 118, 128, 146, 151, 163, 166, 180, 207
Baroda, 16, 23
Basketball, 55, 59, 62, 74
Bhatia, Satish, 31, 65, 195
Bhattacharjee, Dipankar, 128, 130, 163, 195
Binny, Roger, 114

Bisht, Madhumita, 4, 55, 92, 95, 105–106, 110, 130, 132, 138–147, 180
Bombay (now Mumbai), 18–20, 26–28, 35, 38, 40, 58, 66, 80–81, 88–89, 94, 96, 101, 107–108, 113–116, 124–125, 127, 159, 162–163
Bose, Radhika, 106, 110, 195
Boxing, 193, 201, 206

Calcutta, 76, 113, 140, 142–144, 194–195
Chadha, Ashish, 202–203
Chandigarh, 30, 101–102, 104
Chawla, P.P.S., 25–26, 28
China, 80, 116, 122–124, 138, 143, 148–149, 185, 188, 202, 208
Choudhary, Neelima, 132, 165
Crasto, Tanisha, 181
Cricket, 1, 7, 21, 25, 29, 34, 40, 49, 58, 62, 71, 107–108, 113–114, 149–150, 155, 159, 161, 178, 197, 202, 204

Dadar, 107–108
Darjeeling, 138, 142
Delhi, 12, 26, 41, 74, 81, 87, 97–98, 106, 137, 145, 174–177, 186, 194–195, 198
Denmark, 7, 10, 69, 123, 149, 151, 184, 199
Deodhar, Archana, 127, 130
Deodhar sisters, The, 4, 34–36
Deodhar, Suman, 34
Deodhar, Sunder, 34
Deodhar, Tara, 34, 35

Index

Dev, Kapil, 58, 71
Dhillon, Malvinder, 74, 193–195
Diju, 174, 177
Diwan, Amrit Lal, 19, 36
Dongre, Ravindra, 19, 76
D'Sa, Leroy, 4, 112–125, 195–196

Fadnis, Sudhanshu, 208
Fatehgarh Churian, 24
Football, 1, 38, 113–114, 150, 197, 204, 206
Frankfurt, 81
Frost, Mortem, 56, 60, 109

Gandhe, Pradeep, 112–113
Ganguly, Partho, 82, 118, 139
Gavaskar, Sunil, 21, 59, 71, 155, 210
Ghia, Ami, 4, 40, 55–56, 73, 79, 82, 88–96, 105–106, 110, 116, 118, 130, 145–147, 180, 183
Ghosh, Dipu, 30–31, 35, 65, 73, 143, 146, 195
Ghosh, Romen, 35, 39, 65
Goel, Suresh, 4, 20, 28–32, 42–44, 72–73, 111, 115, 146, 195, 200
Gopi Chand, Pullela, 1–2, 6, 22, 50, 52, 54, 75, 122–124, 130–131, 148–158, 165, 174, 179–180, 183, 186–187, 189–190, 199–200, 203, 206
Gorakhpur, 68, 70, 82, 92
Graf, Steffi, 159, 161
Gutta, Jwala, 56, 111, 132, 135–136, 171–181, 196
Guwahati, 19, 40, 91, 209

Hadinata, Christian, 121
Hartono, Rudy, 60, 64–66, 77, 95, 103, 109, 122, 209
Haryana, 99, 187
Hashman, Judy, 44–46
Haughton, Colin, 148
Himachal Pradesh, 104
Hockey, 1, 8, 29, 32, 38, 58, 62, 98, 107–108, 113–114, 150, 178, 197–198, 206

Hussein, Hamid, 151, 153
Hyderabad, 41, 50–51, 61, 91, 113, 121, 131, 150–151, 153, 164, 169, 171, 173, 182–183, 185–186, 192, 200, 207

Indian Railways, 12, 72, 120, 199
Indonesia, 5, 50, 60, 63, 66, 95, 109, 121, 151, 201, 208–209
Intanon, Ratchanok, 6, 186
Ireland, 10, 77

Jabalpur, 66, 100–101, 103
Jain, Sujata, 79, 91
Jaipur, 65, 108, 168
Jakarta, 67, 82, 109, 179
Japan, 179, 202
Jepsen, Conny, 7–9, 21, 29
Jian, Han, 60, 69
JNU, 41, 45

K. D. Singh Babu Stadium, 68, 70, 84
Kanwar, Ajay, 137, 193, 201, 203, 205, 208
Kanwar, Manjusha, 4, 55, 126–137, 154–155, 163–165, 180, 183–184
Kashmir, 13, 97
  Jammu and, 51, 104
Kashyap, Parupalli, 151–152, 186
Kaushik, Kiran, on Prakash Padukone, 62–64
Kelkar, Manda, 20, 38
Khanna, Dinesh, 1, 24–33, 58, 65, 70–71, 105, 195, 200
Kharb, Anmol, 6
Khel Ratna, 154, 184, 192
King, Liem Swie, 50, 57–58, 62, 69, 72, 77, 95, 122
Krishnan, Ramanathan, 22, 29
Krishnan, Ramesh, 72, 201
Kuala Lumpur, 58, 62, 145, 167
Kumar, Manoj, 50, 52
Kumar, Praveen, 50, 52
Kumar, Vimal, 72, 75, 83, 109, 163, 169, 180, 186, 199
Kurien, Shruti, 174, 180–181

Index

Lahore, 7–12, 33
Lakshmi, P. V. V., 128, 135, 145, 164–165, 195
Latif, Rafia, 91, 195
Lewis, George, 7, 29, 114
Li Xuerui, 185–186, 188
London, 4, 7–8, 10, 12, 58, 81, 155, 157, 174, 182, 185, 188
Lucknow, 19, 35–36, 42, 45, 70, 83–85, 189
Luwang, Maisnam Meiraba, 207

Madhya Pradesh, 100–101
Madras, 61, 101
Maharashtra, 14, 19–20, 34, 76, 80–81, 89, 95, 108, 200, 202
Malaysia, 5, 26, 29, 109, 121, 167, 184, 201
Manipur, 206–207
Marin, Carolina, 186, 189–191, 199, 201
Mariska, Gregoria, 186, 189
Mathias, Maureen, 38, 92
Meerut, 98–99
Misra, Sanat, 115, 145
Modi, Syed, 1, 56–57, 60, 62, 68–75, 77, 80–85, 87, 95, 150, 189, 200
Mohan, Devinder, 7, 9–10, 29

Nadkarni, Shirish, 7, 11, 16–18, 21–22, 44, 57–58, 61, 69, 72, 78–79, 90, 115–116, 120, 125, 160, 169, 174, 210
Nariman, Hufrish, 40, 107–111, 118, 177
Natekar, Nandu, 1, 4, 14–23, 26–27, 30–31, 35–36, 39–40, 44, 114, 200, 210
Nath, Ashok, 9, 11
Nath, Prakash, 4, 7–13, 29, 149
Nath, Ratna, 9–12
Nehwal, Saina, 3–4, 40, 46, 50, 52, 54, 78, 133, 135–136, 151–152, 157–158, 166, 169, 175, 182–187, 191–192, 200–202, 204–205
Noida, 201, 205

Ooi, Teik Hok, 29

Padma Bhushan, 187, 192
Padma Shri, 146–147, 187, 192
Padukone, Prakash, 1–2, 12, 22, 55–75, 77, 82–83, 95, 115, 119, 122–123, 128, 139, 141, 146, 148–150, 155, 161, 163, 165, 167, 169–171, 178, 183–184, 191, 193–196, 198–200, 205, 207
Pakistan, 8, 12, 24, 41, 61
Park, Joo-Bong, 121
Patiala, 73, 110, 118, 209
Pawar, Uday, 60, 118–119, 127, 131, 195–196
Ponnappa, Ashwini, 171, 174, 178–181, 196
Popat, Aparna, 4, 55, 131–132, 135, 147, 159, 160–170
Pradhan, Anil, 116, 159–161, 164–165
Praneeth, B. Sai, 158, 205
Prannoy, H. S., 158, 204–205
Pune, 38, 126, 137, 161, 206
Punjab, 24–26, 28–29, 33, 97, 101, 103, 116, 128
Puri, T. P., 131

Rajasthan, 65, 97
Rajgopal, Dr Ashok, 156
Ramana, P. V., 3, 188–189, 191
Rankireddy, Satwiksairaj, 5, 125, 179–180, 196, 203–205
Rege, Sushila, 35, 40
Rome, 10, 81
Ruia, Ramnarain, 20

Sangli, 14
Sen, Lakshya, 5, 203–205
Seth, Trilok Nath, 4, 19, 26–27, 35–36, 195
Siliguri, 138–139, 141–142

Index

Sindhu, P. V., 3–4, 6, 40, 46–47, 50, 54–55, 133, 135–136, 146, 151–152, 158, 179, 185–186, 188–192, 200–201, 204–205
Singh, Ameeta, 73–74, 76–87
Singh, K. D., 32–33
Singh, Kanwal Thakar, 39, 56, 91–94, 97–106, 112, 118
Singh, Mrs Thakar, 98, 100–102
Singh, Sanjay, 84, 86
Shah, Meena, 4, 35–37, 39–40, 46–47, 55, 90, 92, 110–111
Shahjahanabad, 97
Sharma, Sanjay, 60–61, 73, 93, 105, 113, 153, 187, 191
Shetty, Chirag, 5, 60, 125, 180, 196, 203–205
Shobha, 37–40, 46, 91–92, 195
Sportstar, 1, 3, 58, 70, 147, 154, 179, 181–182, 186, 190
Squash, 47, 97–98
Srikanth, Kidambi, 5, 158, 205, 207
Soon, Wong Peng, 21
Spain, 189, 201
Subrahmanyam, V. V., 3, 50, 156–158, 171, 177, 180–181, 187, 192
Suri, Santosh, 70, 72–75
Swimming, 76, 98, 100, 126, 129–130, 173, 178

Table tennis, 9, 38, 43, 59, 77, 113, 121, 159, 161, 173, 205
Tai Tzu Ying, 186, 201
Tambay, Damayanti, 37, 39, 41–48, 90, 110–111
Tambay, Vijay, 41, 48
Target Olympic Podium Scheme (TOPS), 4–5, 206, 208
Thailand, 6, 32, 36, 186
Thakkar, Gautam, 17, 116
Thanekar, Deepti, 79, 126, 132
The Hindu, 1, 3, 69
Thyagarajan, S., 1–2, 69
Training age, The, 52–53

US, The (*also* America), 35, 80, 106
Usha, P. T., 71, 161
Uttar Pradesh, 36, 73, 81, 87, 98

Vijaya, 3, 191
Vijayawada, 50, 56, 68–69
Volleyball, 3, 94, 138, 188, 192, 198

Wang Xin, 185
Wang Yihan, 185
West Bengal, 104, 138, 147
Wrestling, 193, 201

Zurich, 81

About the Authors

Akshay Lokapally, a science graduate from Ramjas College with experience in the field of education, has not only pursued his passion for reading but also shared his knowledge through his contributions to various publications. This is his debut book, highlighting his dedication to the field.

Vijay Lokapally is a retired sports journalist who worked with *The Hindu* and *Sportstar*. He is the author of the bestselling *Driven: The Virat Kohli Story*, published by Bloomsbury.